CANADA

Explore past and present maps of Canada
through these provocative map games and puzzles—
all designed for mastering map skills.

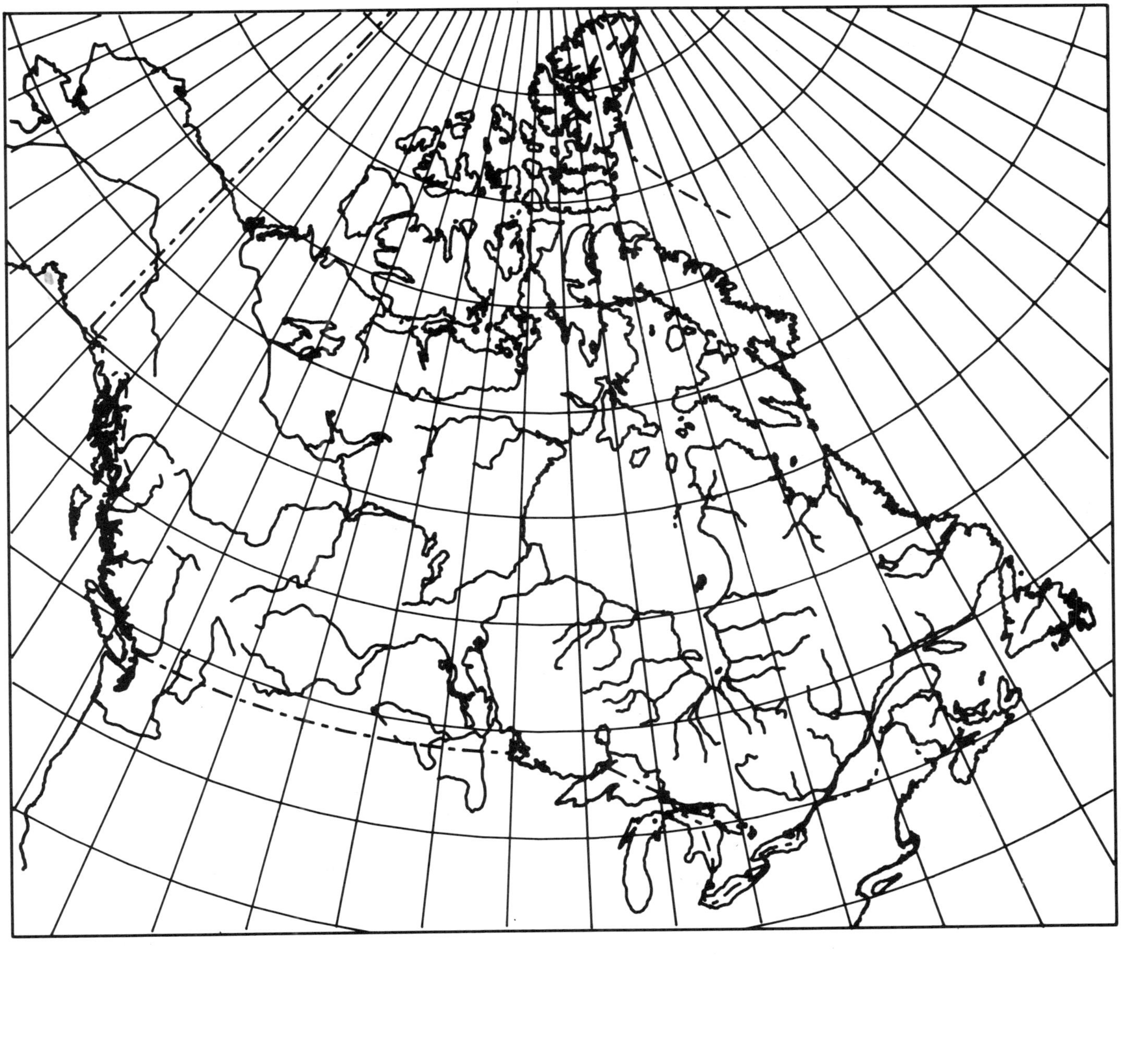

Mastering Map Skills

The best way to master map skills is through the use of maps. But before you can use maps effectively, you must know **how** to interpret the information they contain. Also, a good way to learn more about a country is by examining its maps. To help you better understand some of Canada's history and geography, this book includes a variety of map examples from across Canada.

There are many different kinds of maps: relief or physical maps, land-use maps, and route maps, to name a few. However, basic information in all maps is obtained through their symbols and scale. Such information must be interpreted correctly in order to understand both the purpose and message of the map.

Map symbols are usually explained in a legend or key. Symbols can show physical features such as islands or rivers. Symbols can also show cultural features such as roads or towns by recording how people have changed the landscape. Map symbols, like the key words in a story or message, reveal what is important on the map.

Maps also include information about direction and scale. A compass rose indicates the north direction. Grid lines or lines of latitude and longitude give the position of places. The map scale tells how much the map has been reduced in size compared to the part of the earth that the map represents. These things help you compare the shapes and sizes of features on different maps. Knowing how to use the map scale enables you to measure distances accurately and calculate area.

As you learn to interpret a variety of map symbols and shapes, determine direction and position, and measure distances and area using scale, your ability to recognize and interpret important information on maps improves. Maps then become more understandable and also more useful learning tools.

The activities in this book will help you learn more about Canada's history and geography and also provide a method to help you master important map skills in a sequential, cumulative, and enjoyable way.

Published in Canada by **Apple Press**, 49 Apple Orchard Path, Thornhill, Ontario L3T 3B5

ISBN 0-919972-20-9

Contents

Canada

Recognizing Shape

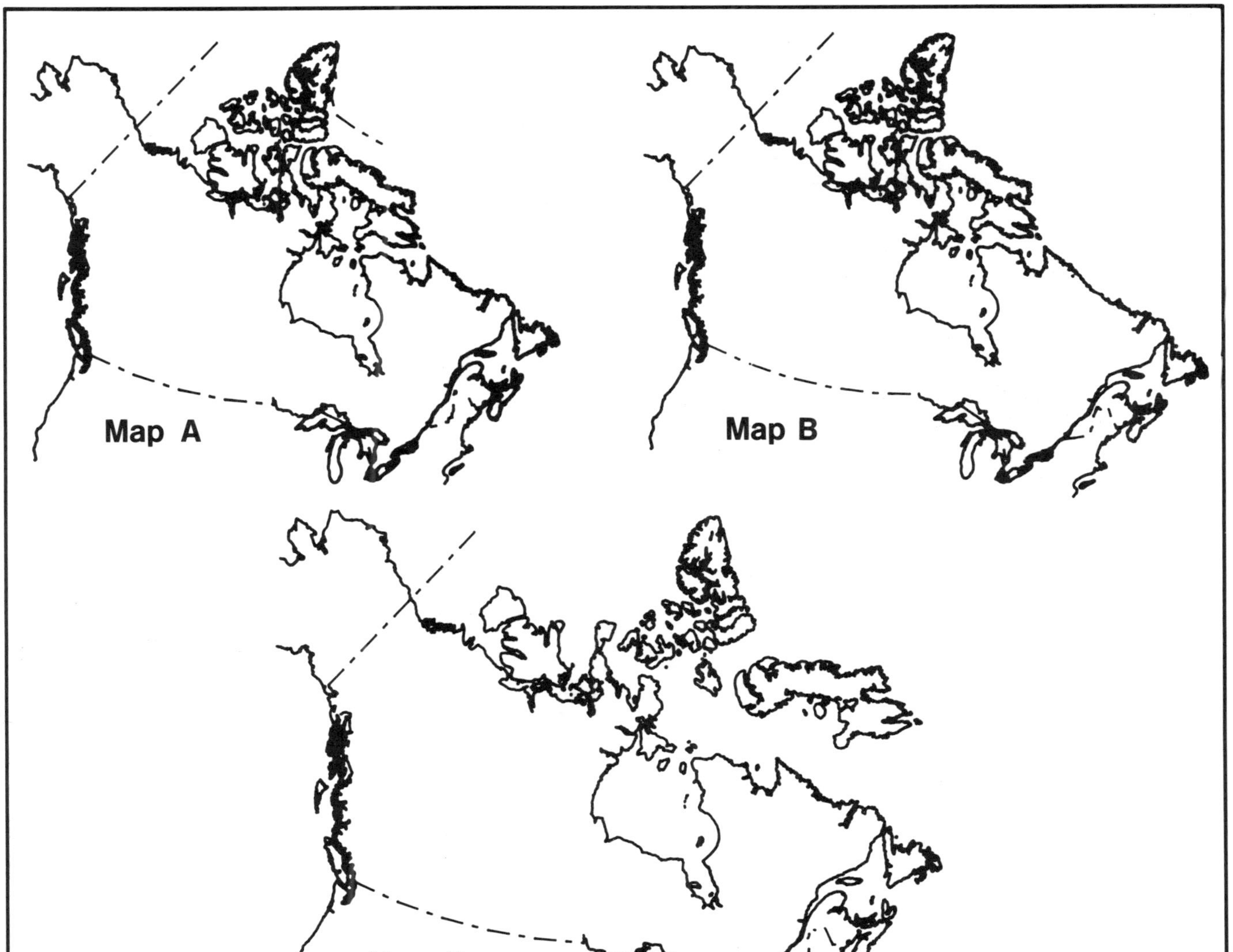

Which shape of Canada is the correct one?

Recognizing Shapes from Above

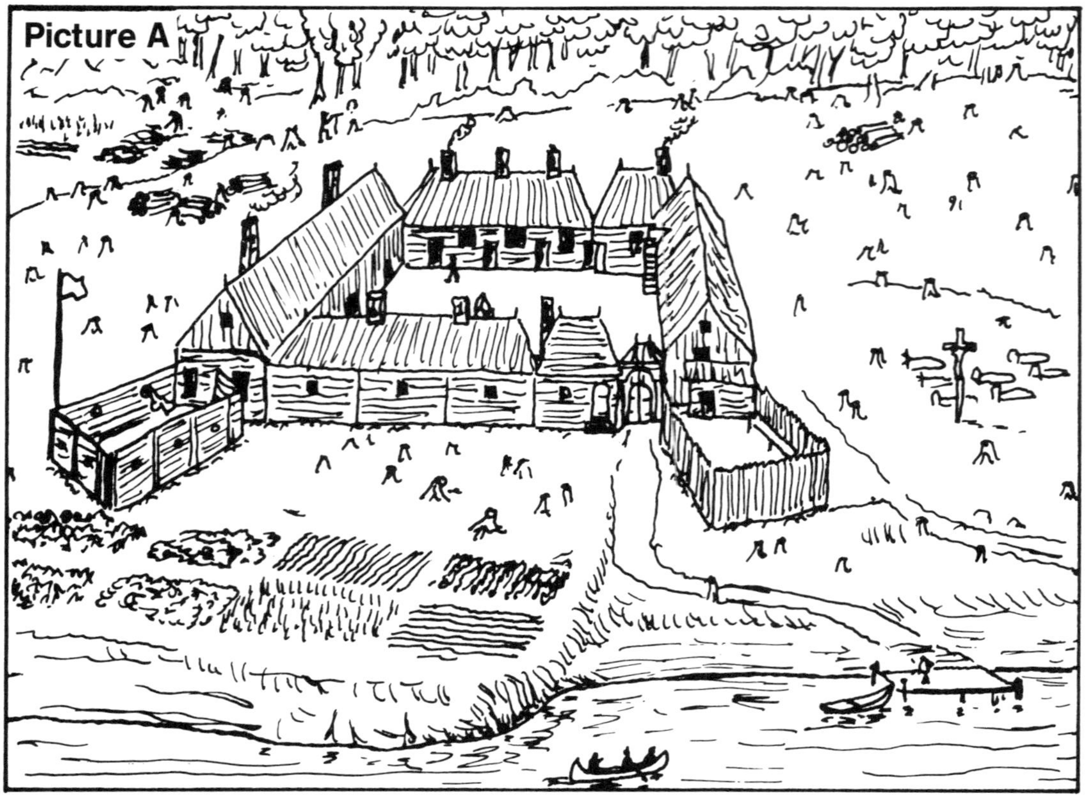

Does Picture **B** or **C** show the correct overhead view of Port Royal?

Find and circle the five mistakes in the other picture.

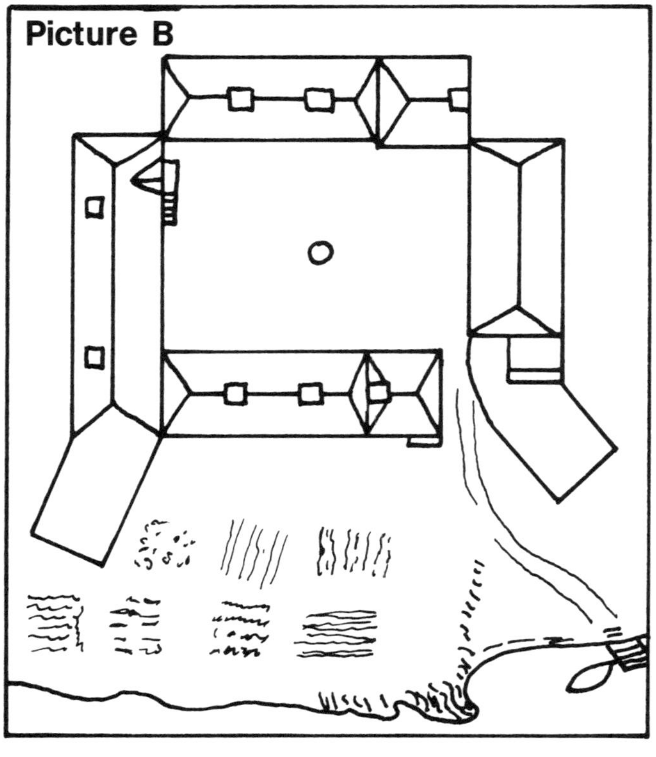

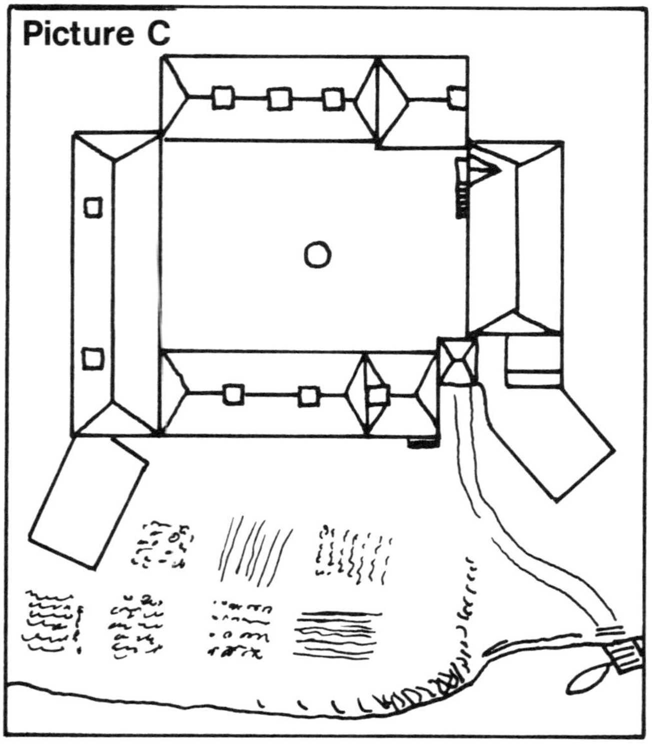

Recognizing Shapes on a Map

Port Royal was one of the first European settlements in Canada. This small, wooden fort, or habitation, was established in 1605 by Samuel de Champlain and his friend, Sieur de Monts. It was built after an earlier colony on the nearby Île-Ste-Croix had failed.

Port Royal was constructed close to the Bay of Fundy in Acadia, at the mouth of the Dauphin River. There, the tiny settlement was close to a supply of fresh water and a safe harbour. All around, the land was fertile and covered with thick forests. It was also protected from the cold, north winds by low hills.

But Port Royal as a fur trading post was too far away from the growing fur trade of the interior of New France. In 1607, Port Royal was abandoned. One year later, in 1608, Champlain established another habitation in the St. Lawrence Valley at the site of Quebec. To-day, a replica or model showing what Port Royal once looked like, stands on its original site in the Annapolis Valley of Nova Scotia.

PORT ROYAL

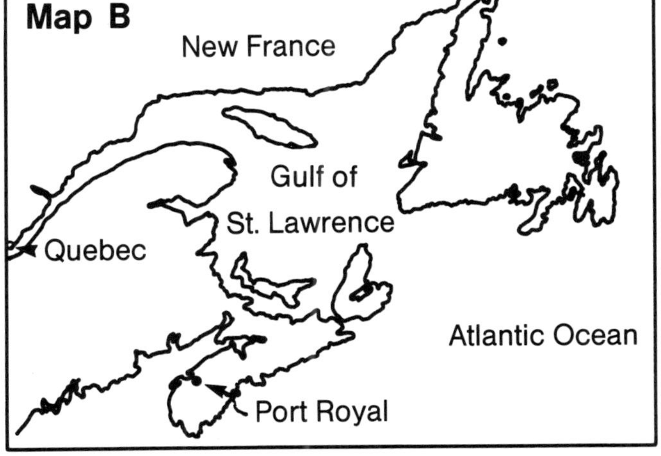

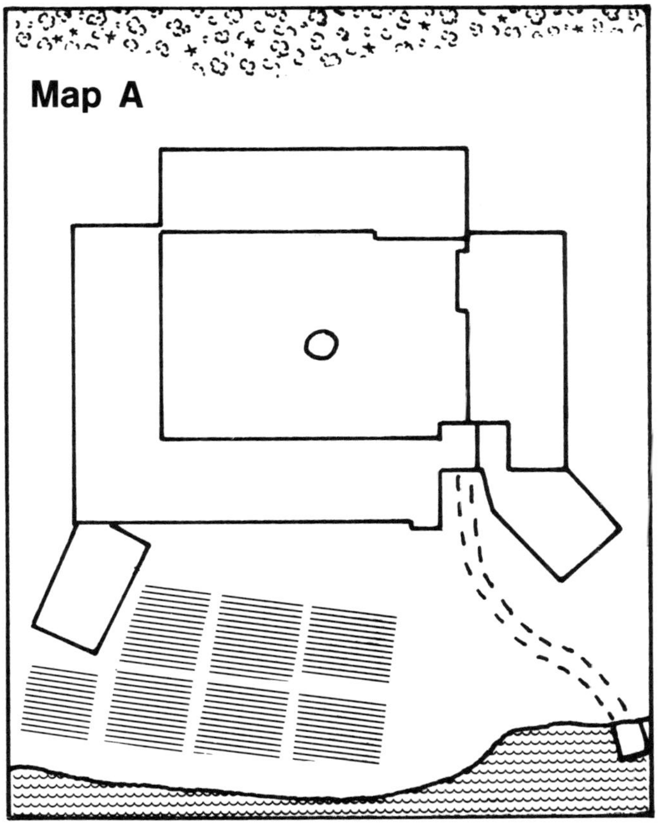

A map is like a picture of the earth's surface seen from space. Maps reveal the shapes of important things on the earth seen from straight above, and show features in two dimensions—length and width. Depth is not shown, so things look flat on a map.

1. Colour Map **A** to show:
   water—blue
   trees, forest—green
   cleared land—brown
   buildings—choose a colour
2. Two ways in which Map **A** is like an overhead or top view:

   ____

   ____

3. Two ways in which Map **A** is different from the top view:

   ____

   ____

   ____

Comparing Shapes on a Map and on a Globe

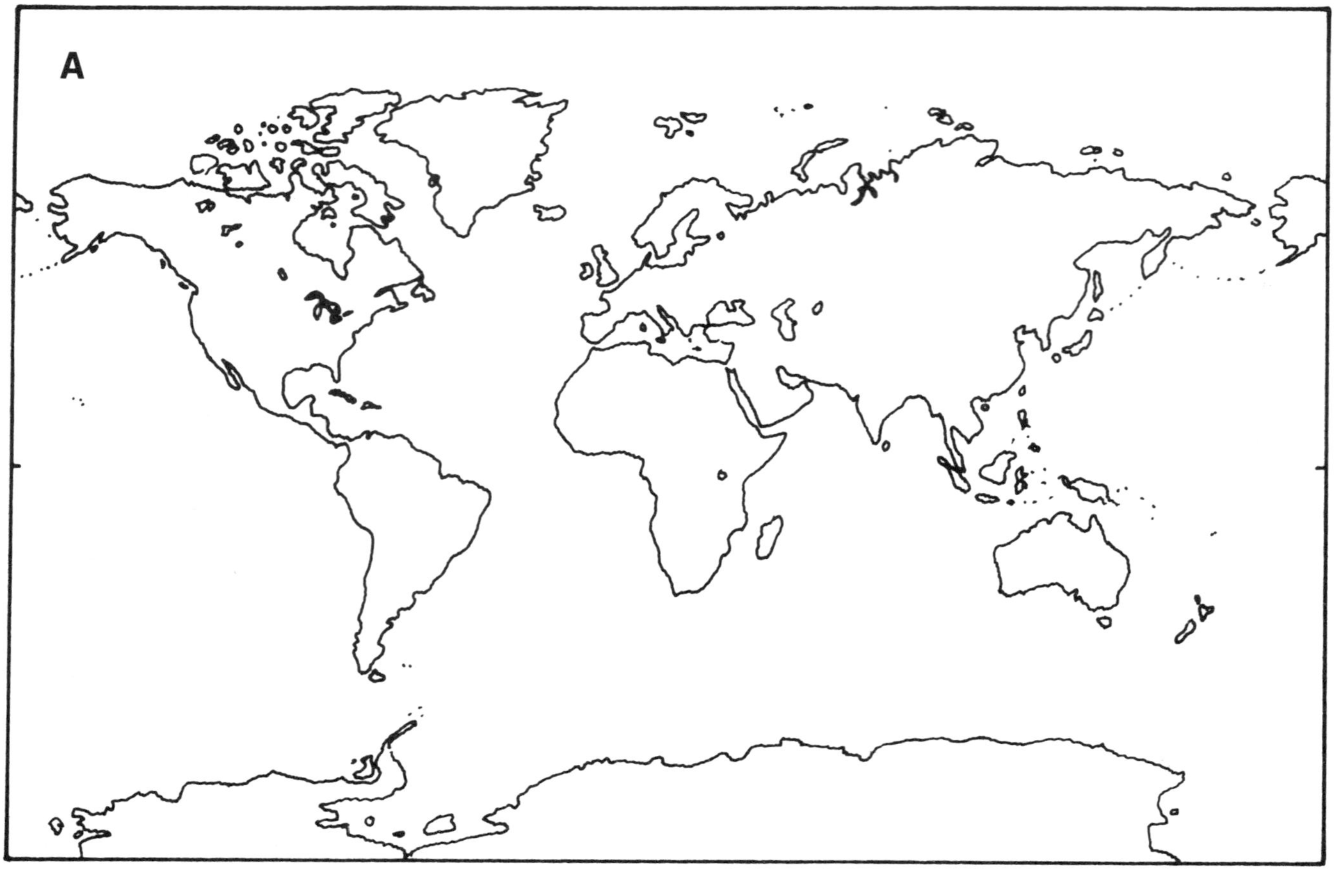

1. Which view of the world is a map view? ______________________

   Shade in the land area.

2. The other view is called a global view.

   Shade in the land area.

3. The earth is a sphere. The globe is also a sphere. A globe is the most accurate way to show the shapes of land and water areas. Colour North America on both the map and the globe.

4. a) Does the map or the globe let you see the whole world at once?

   b) Which would be more easily carried or stored? Why?

   c) Which could be more easily enlarged to show a small area in detail?

5. An imaginary line, the equator, divides the globe into two equal parts—northern hemisphere and southern hemisphere. Draw this line on the map.

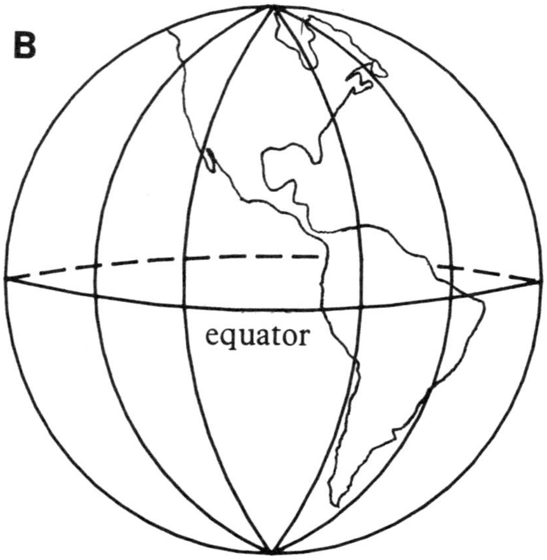

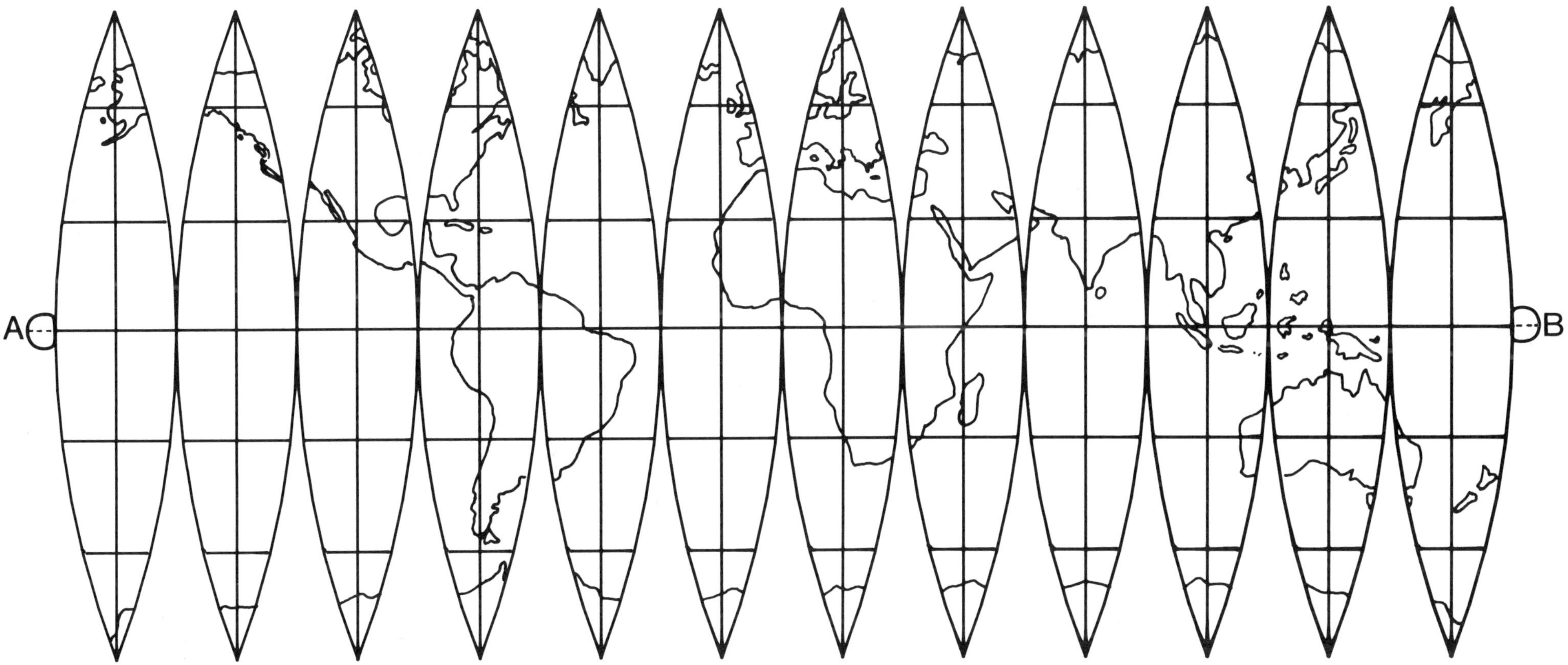

Constructing a Paper Globe

You will need: coloured pencils or markers, string, tape or glue, scissors, ruler.

a) Label the equator, line **A-B**.

b) Name and colour the land and water areas.

c) Use scissors to cut out the map segments. Be careful not to cut too close to the equator.

d) Tape or glue together ends **A** and **B**.

e) Carefully fold the tips of the segments together and fasten them with glue or tape. These will become the poles.

f) Tape some string to the top of the globe.

g) Hang up your new globe and admire it!

Identifying the Shape of Continents and Oceans

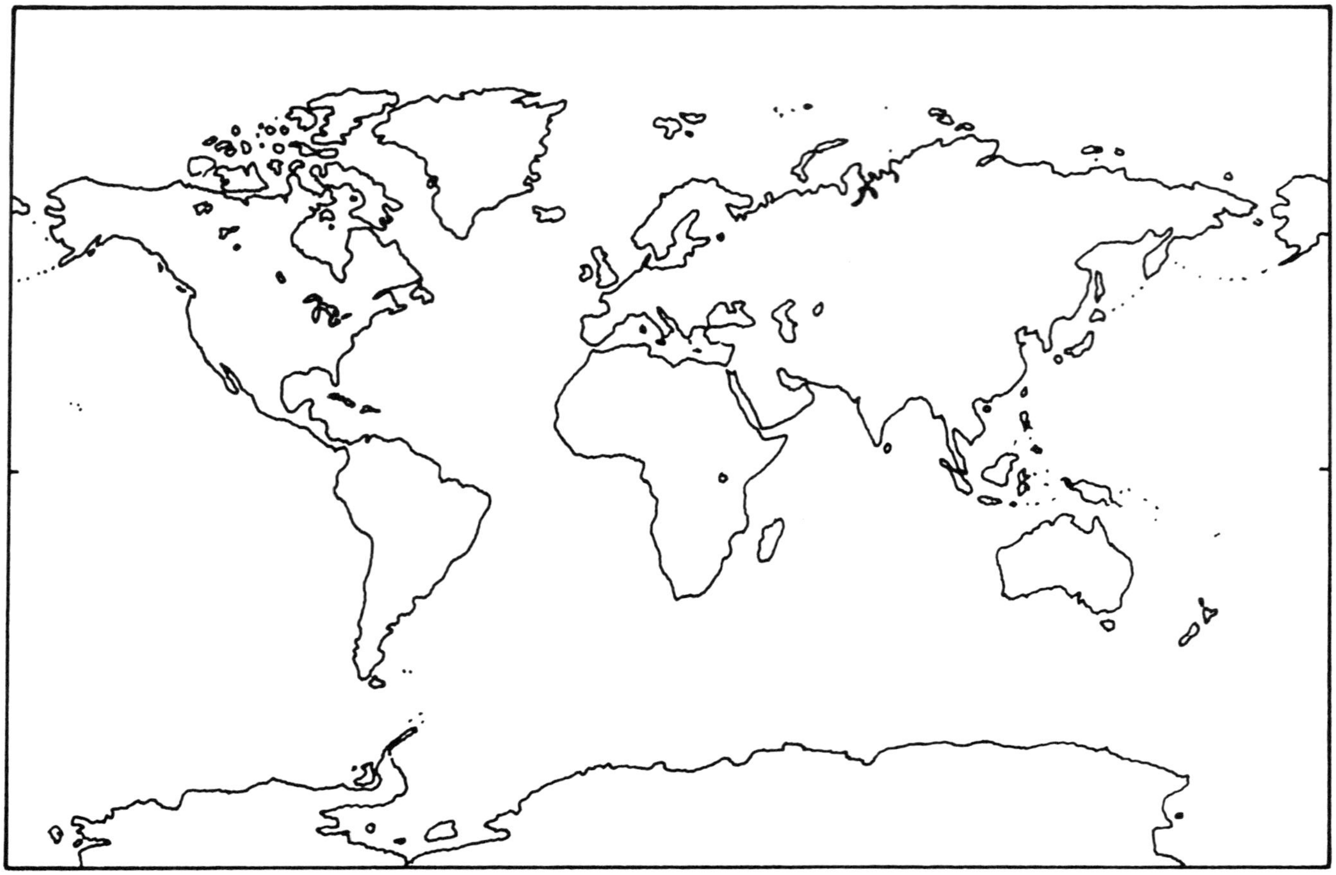

1. Print the name of each continent in its correct place on the map.
   North America
   South America
   Africa
   Australia
   Asia
   Antarctica
   Europe
2. Print the name of each ocean in its correct place on the map.
   Atlantic
   Arctic
   Indian
   Pacific
3. Mark the equator on the map. The equator is an imaginary line that

   ____

   ______________________________.

4. The equator crosses these two continents:

   ____

   ____

5. Which continent is closest to the North Pole?

   ____

6. Name the continent on which you live.

   ____

Recognizing Distortion of Maps

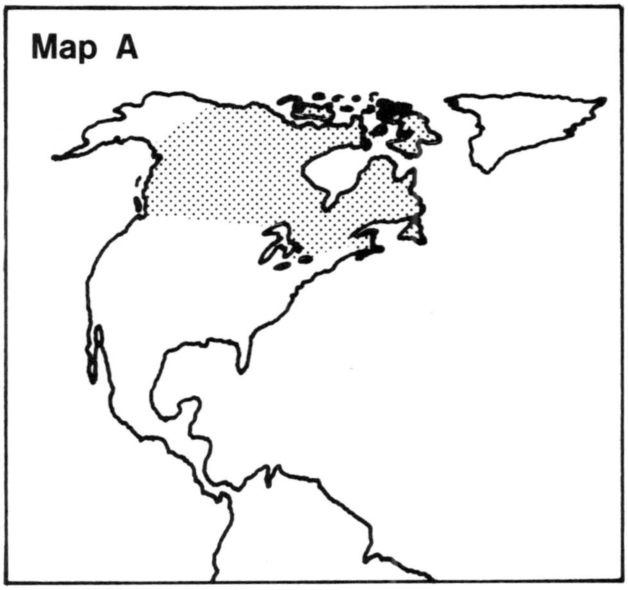

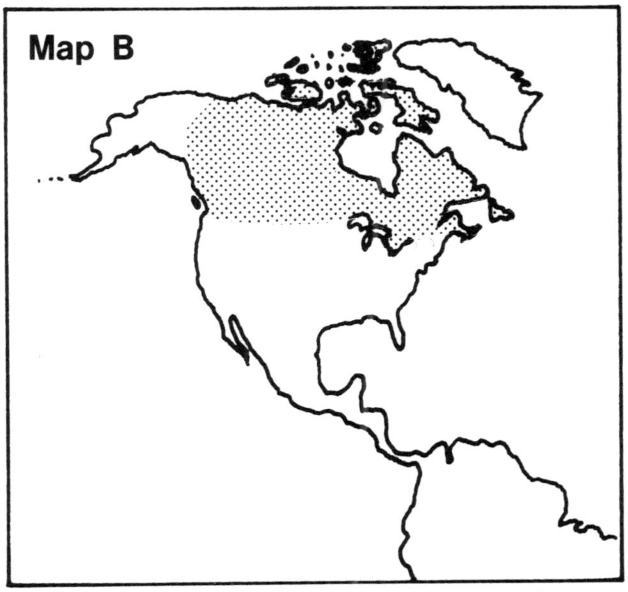

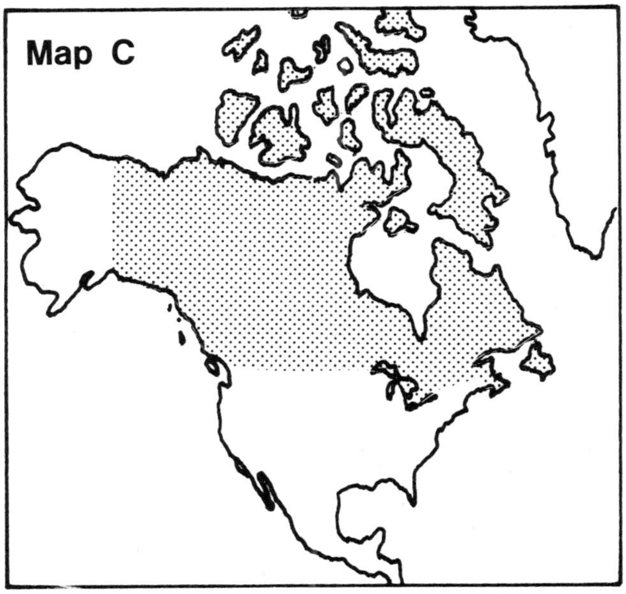

1. Maps **A, B,** and **C** each show the shape of Canada and North America. In which ways are the three maps different?

____

____.

2. A flat map represents a part of the earth's surface that is curved. Either the shape, or the area is not exactly correct on a map. This is why a flat map cannot be a truly accurate representation of the curved surface of the earth. Which map of Canada, **A, B,** or **C** looks most accurate in shape?

____.

3. Find out the meaning of **distortion.** How could you represent large masses of land and water without distorting their shape and their area?

____

____.

4. Name certain kinds of charts and maps where the **shape** of the land and water have to be shown accurately and without distortion.

____

____

____.

5. Name some kinds of maps that would have to show **area** accurately and without distortion.

____

____

____.

Hidden Shapes

Hidden in this map of Canada are:

a standing fox,
a flying goose,
and a plump rabbit.

Can you find them all?

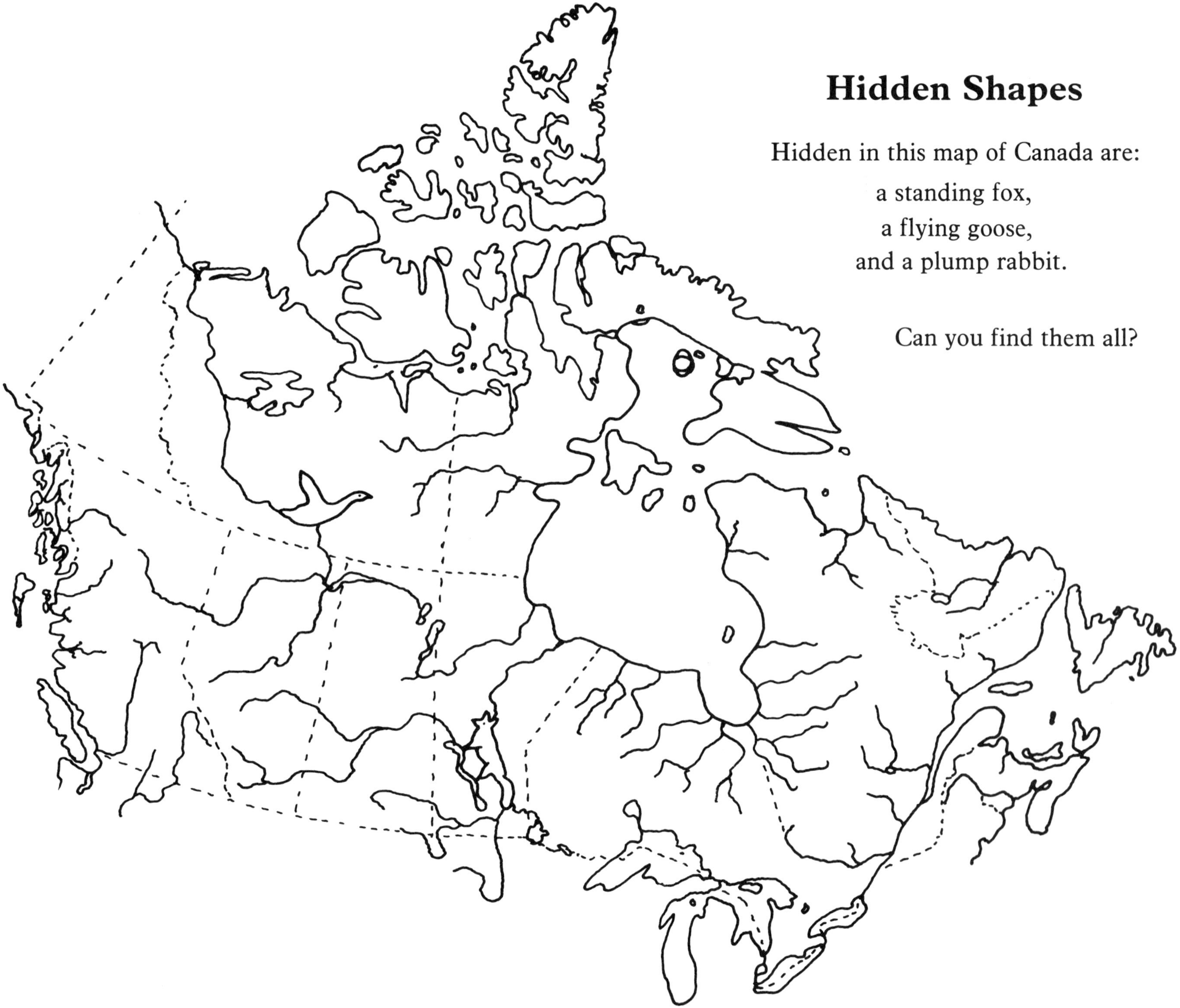

Missing Shapes

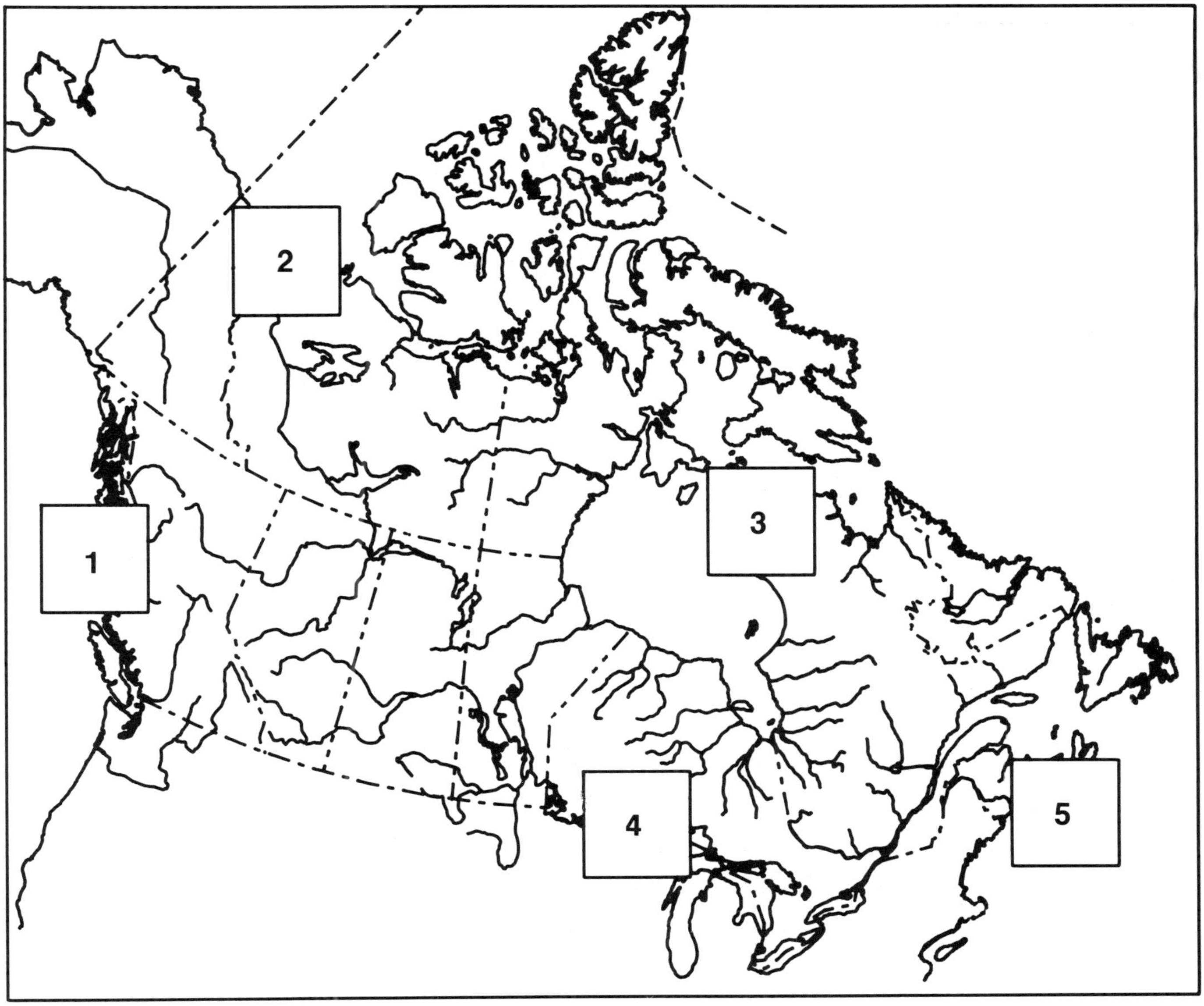

Complete the above outline map by putting five of the squares below in their proper place on the map. Turn some of the squares to help you.

You will not need one of the squares.

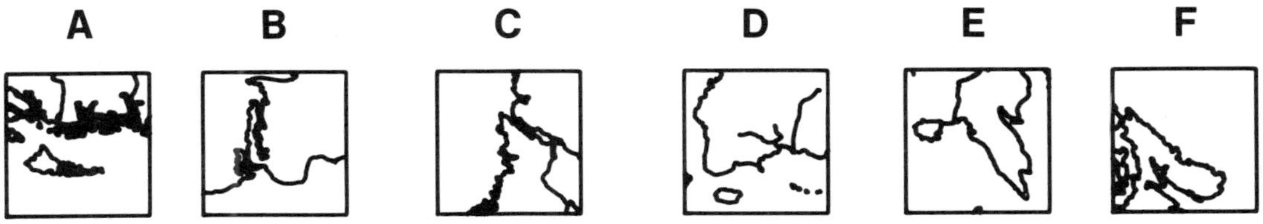

Recognizing the Shape of the Provinces

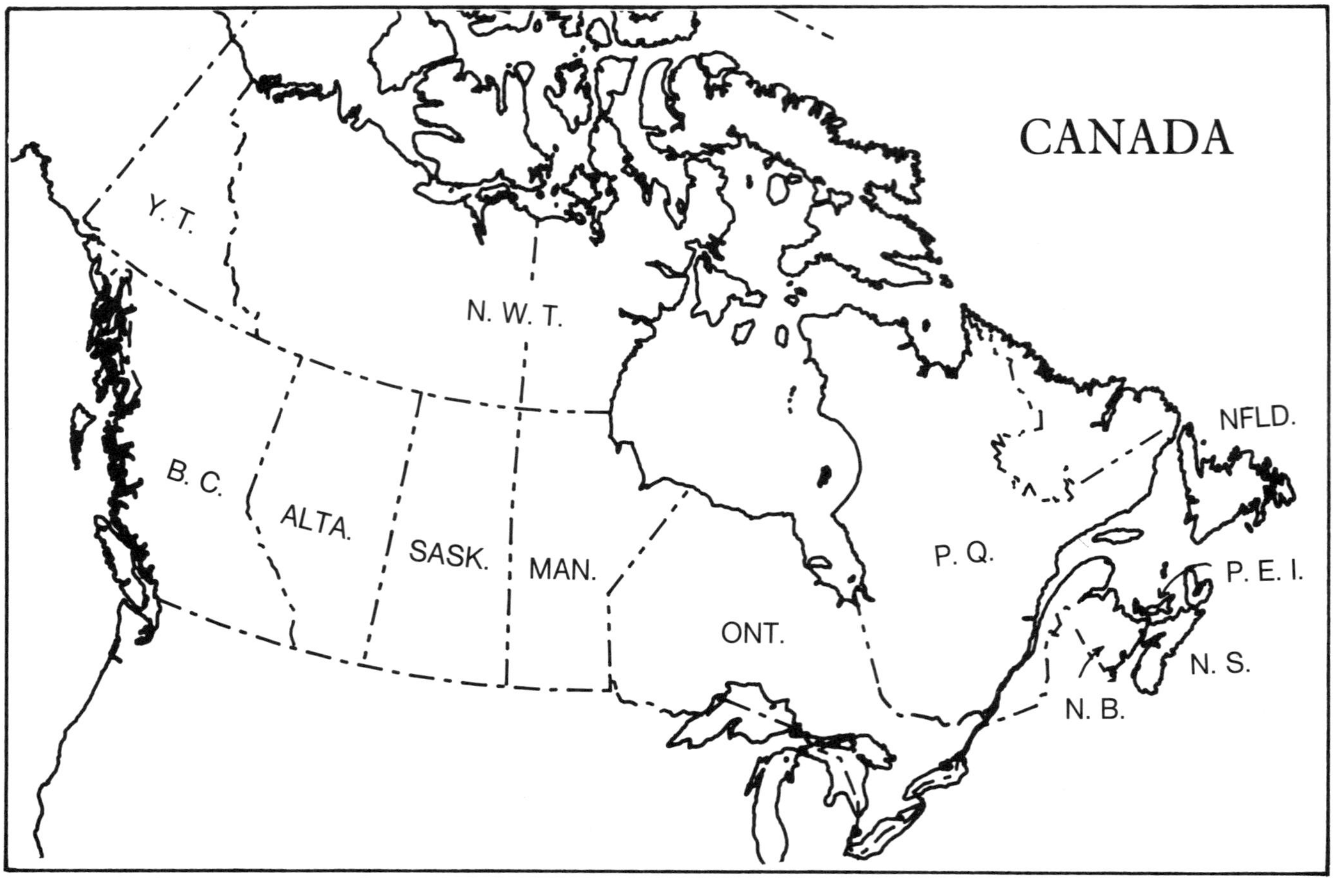

Some of the shapes in the box below are shown larger or smaller than they are on the above map. Shade in only those provinces whose **shape,** not size, correctly matches their shape on the map.

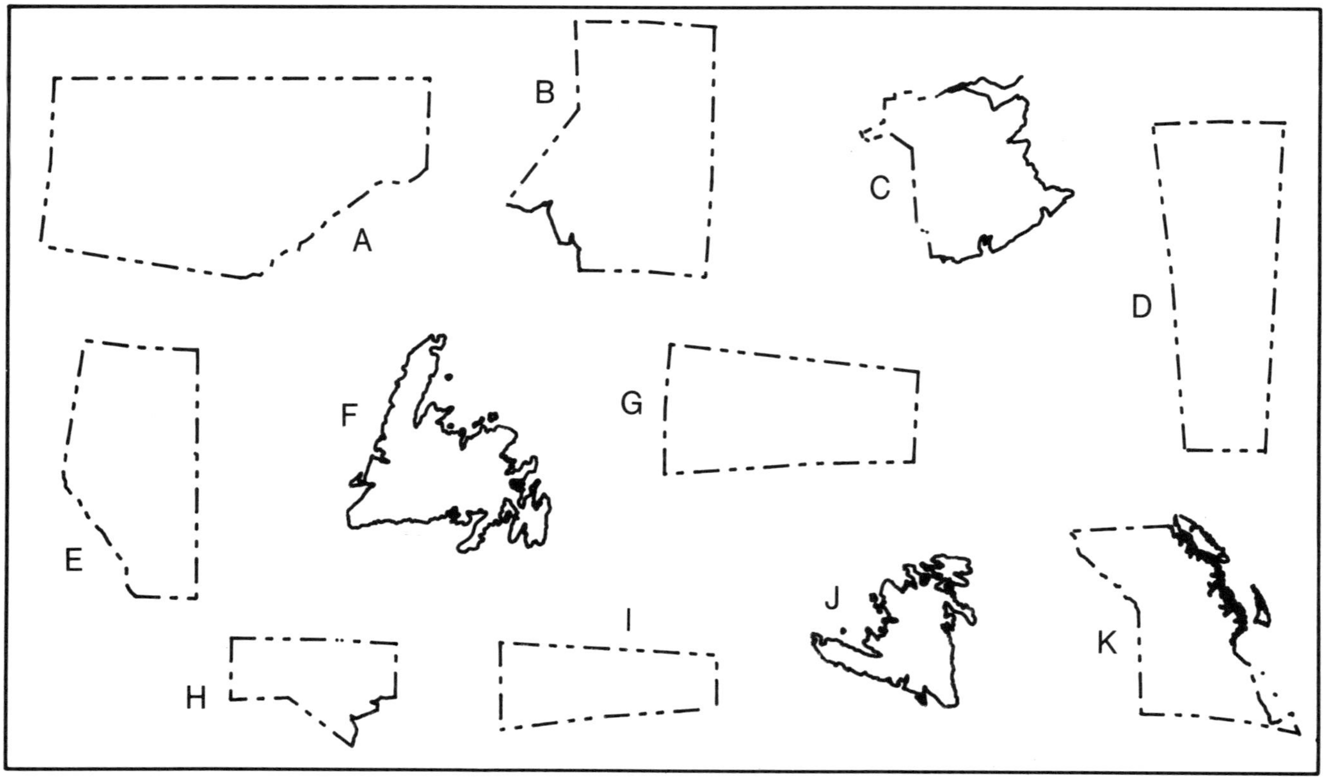

Recognizing the Shape of Some Water Bodies

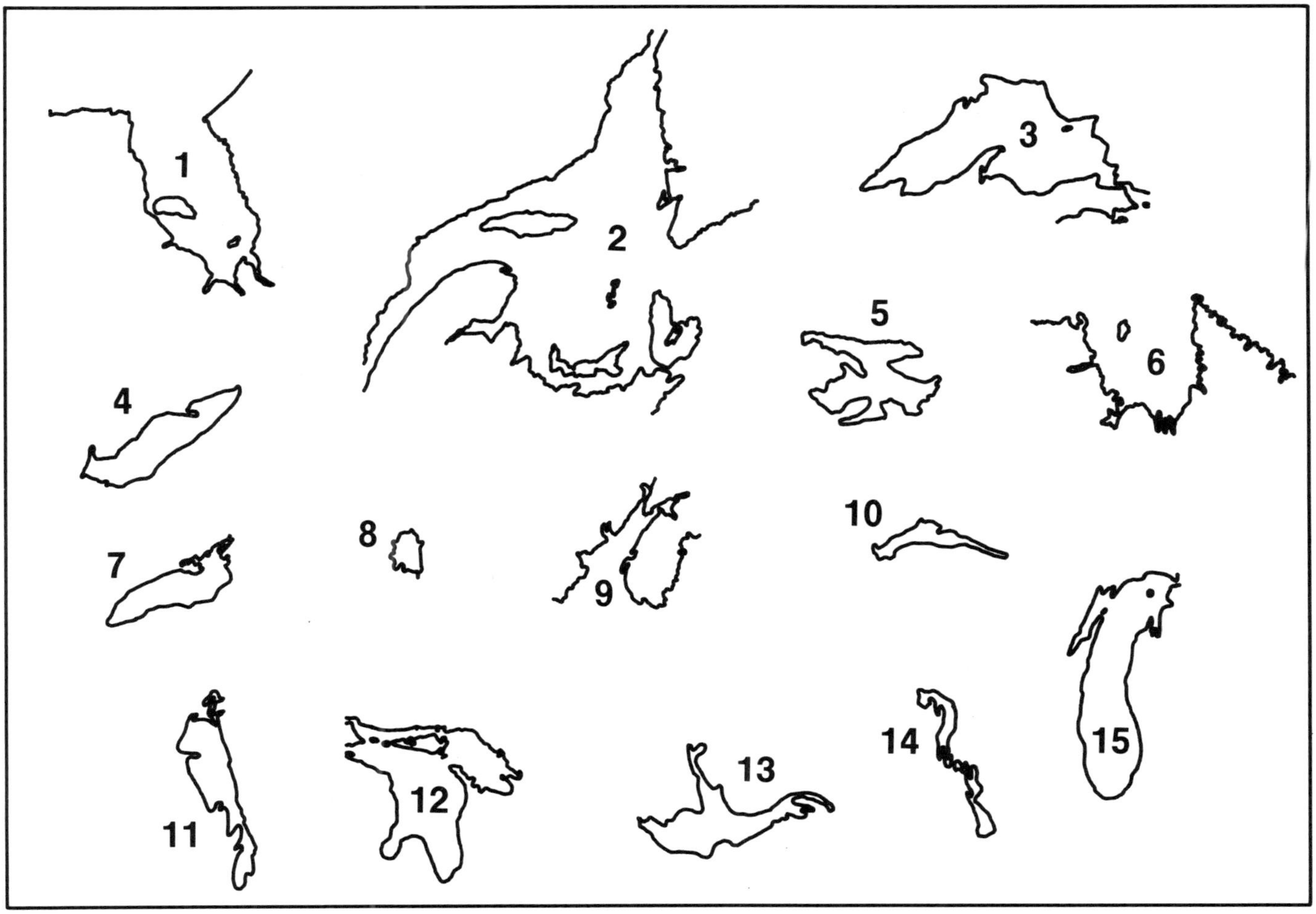

Using the above shapes as a clue, identify these lakes and other bodies of water within Canada.

1 ______________________

2 ______________________

3 ______________________

4 ______________________

5 ______________________

6 ______________________

7 ______________________

8 ______________________

9 ______________________

10 ______________________

11 ______________________

12 ______________________

13 ______________________

14 ______________________

15 ______________________

The Changing Shape of North America

The shape of the earth's land masses has changed many times during the last billion years. The continent of North America had already formed 150 million years ago. At that time, large mountain ranges stood where Hudson Bay is now located. To the west, the land that is presently part of the Rocky Mountains was under ancient seas.

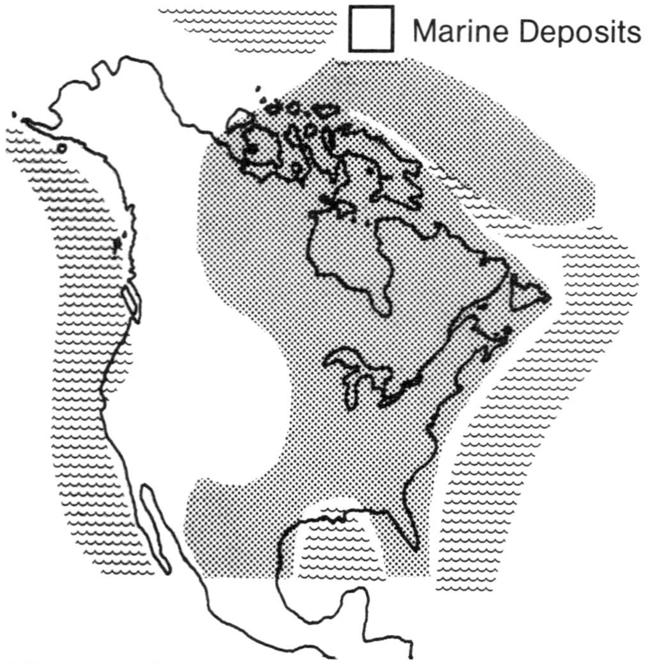

150 MILLION YEARS AGO

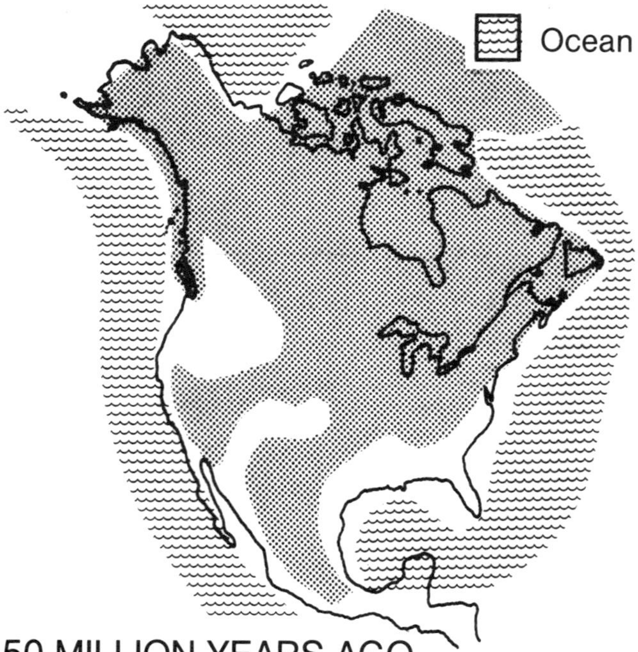

50 MILLION YEARS AGO

Since those prehistoric times, powerful forces have continued to slowly but constantly build up and wear away the land. During mountain-building times, pressure from within the earth caused the land to crack or fault. Molten rock from deep inside the earth was forced to the surface to form volcanoes. Parts of the earth's crust became bent or folded. These building-up forces were uneven and occurred over millions of years.

As the land was raised above sea level, other forces wore away and weakened the newly-exposed rock. Such weathered rocks were gradually carried away or eroded by moving water (waves and rivers), moving ice (glaciers), and wind. Over time, these forces of weathering and erosion wore down the high land to low, flat plains. Large quantities of rock pieces and sand were carried out to sea and deposited on the sea floor.

The weight of the sand, clay, and other material on the ocean floor again forced up molten rock from deep within the earth's crust. It broke through the weakest parts of the crust to create more new mountains. So the cycle of building up and wearing away goes on. This is why the shape of North America continues to slowly, but constantly change.

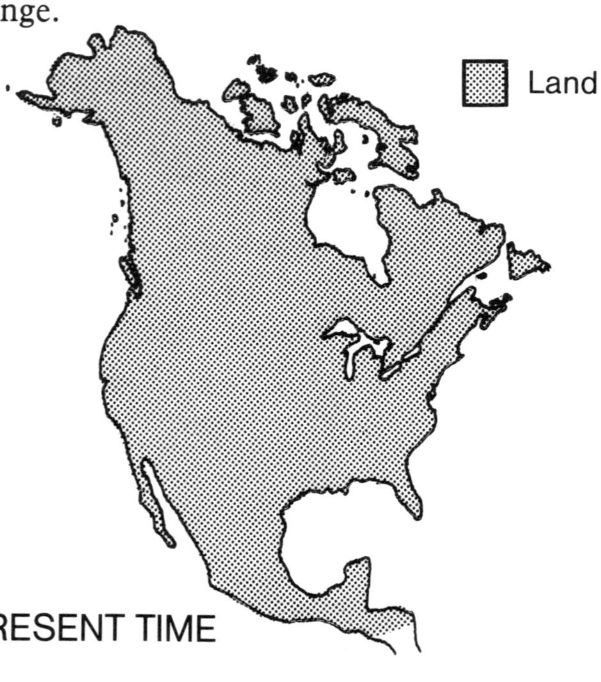

PRESENT TIME

Word Search

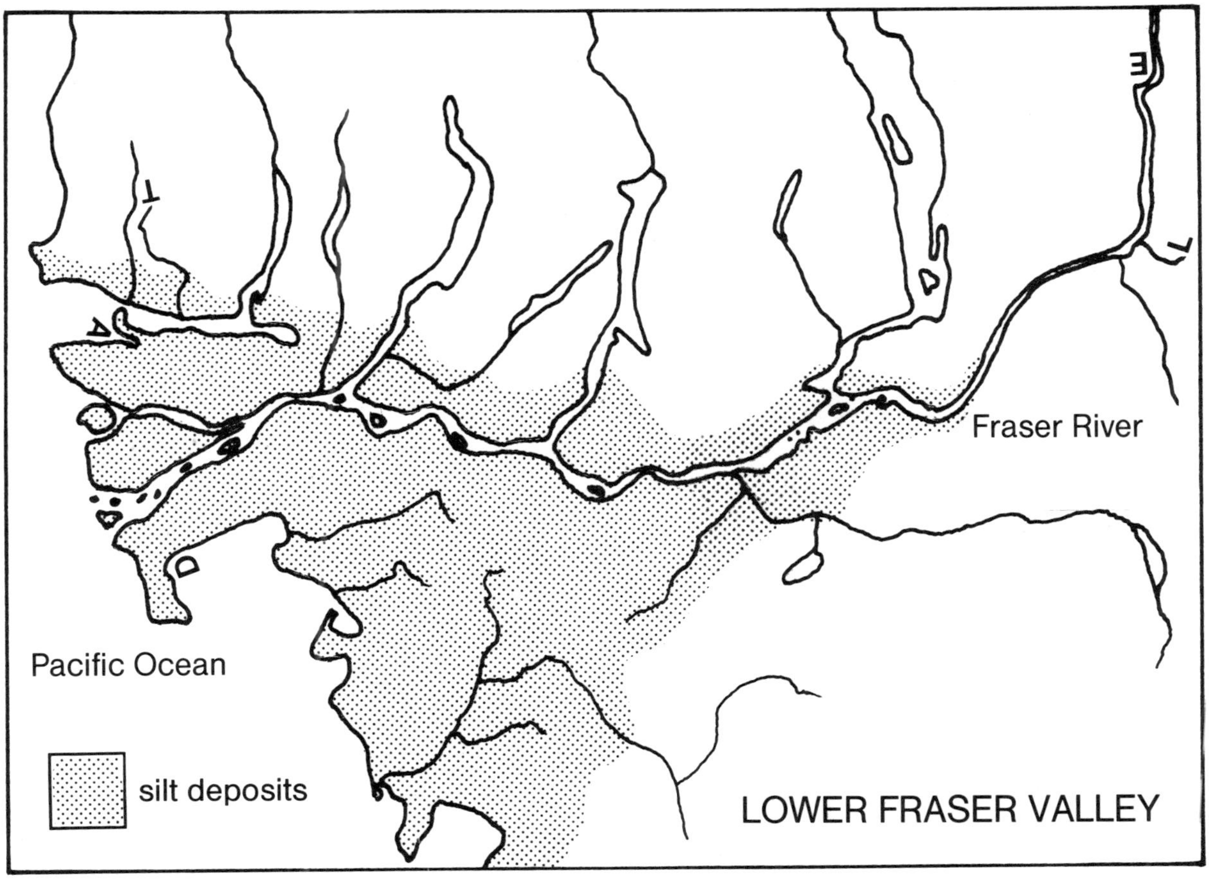

The map shows part of the Fraser River where it empties into the Pacific Ocean. As this river flows swiftly through the Interior and Coast Mountains, it carries along small stones, sand, and mud. When the river reaches the sea, the speed of the water slows down, and these tiny particles settle to the bottom. Over time, these deposits, called silt, form flat and fertile land. Such deposits gradually grow in size and often change the shape of the river's mouth. Land formed from silt that has been carried by a river and deposited at its mouth is called a

___ ___ ___ ___ ___ .

Clue: The five letters that make up this word are hidden somewhere in the map.

Canada Crossword

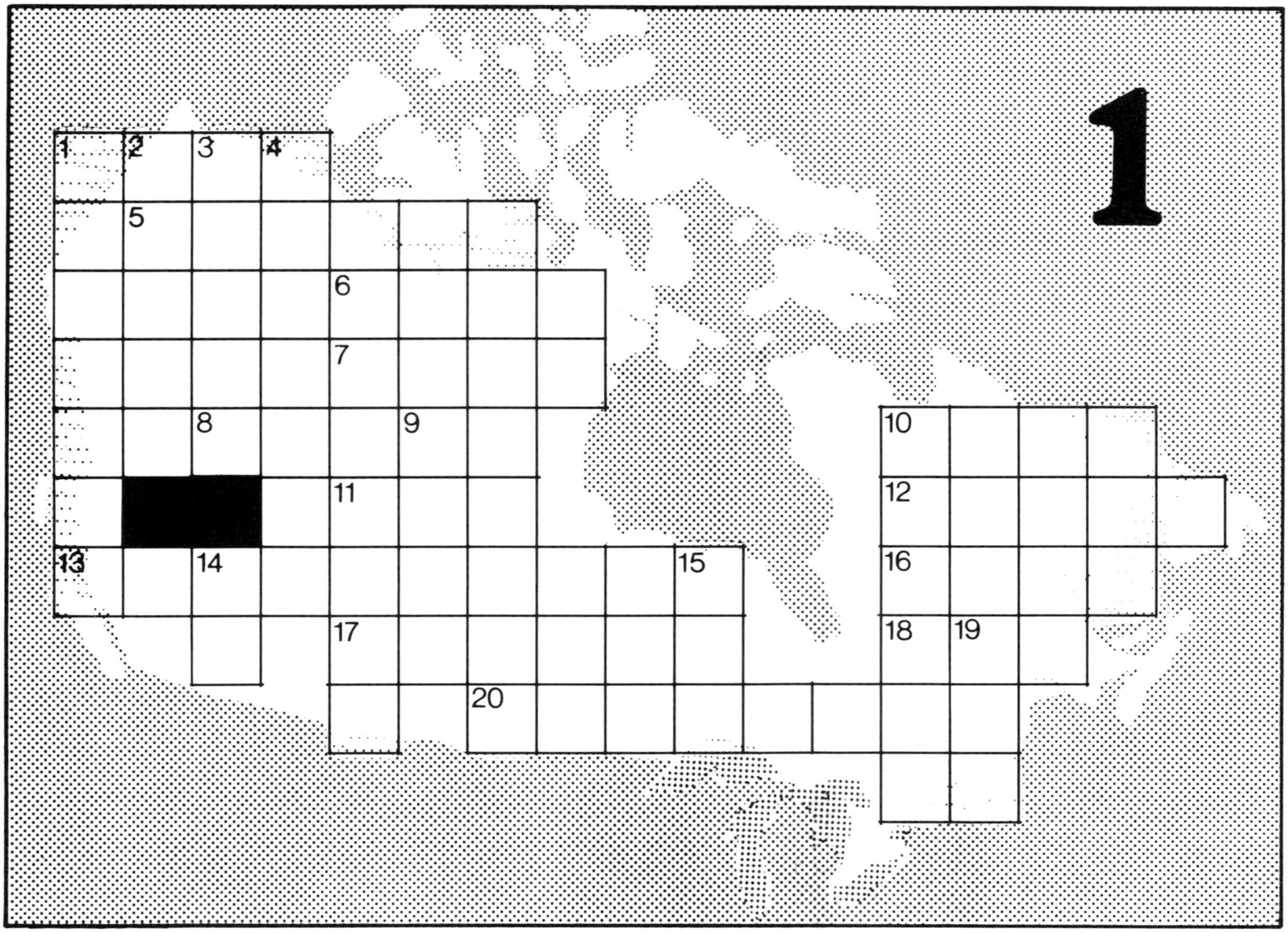

ACROSS

1 Most northern or southern point of the globe

5 Large country just north of the United States

6 Direction of the sunrise

7 To wander

8 Sphere with a map of the world on it

10 Another word for region

12 Large stream of water flowing into another body of water

13 One of the earth's seven great land masses

16 Point of land, a peninsula

17 Capital city of Canada

18 Highest point or part

20 Capital city of British Columbia

DOWN

1 Ocean between Asia and the Americas

2 A very large body of salt water

3 Solid part of the earth's surface

4 To make able, to authorize

6 The process of being worn away gradually

9 Not straight, made crooked or curved

10 North polar region

14 Short form for New Brunswick

15 Small, flat piece of material used as a floor covering

19 Pole with a flat blade at one end for rowing or steering

Determining Position and Direction

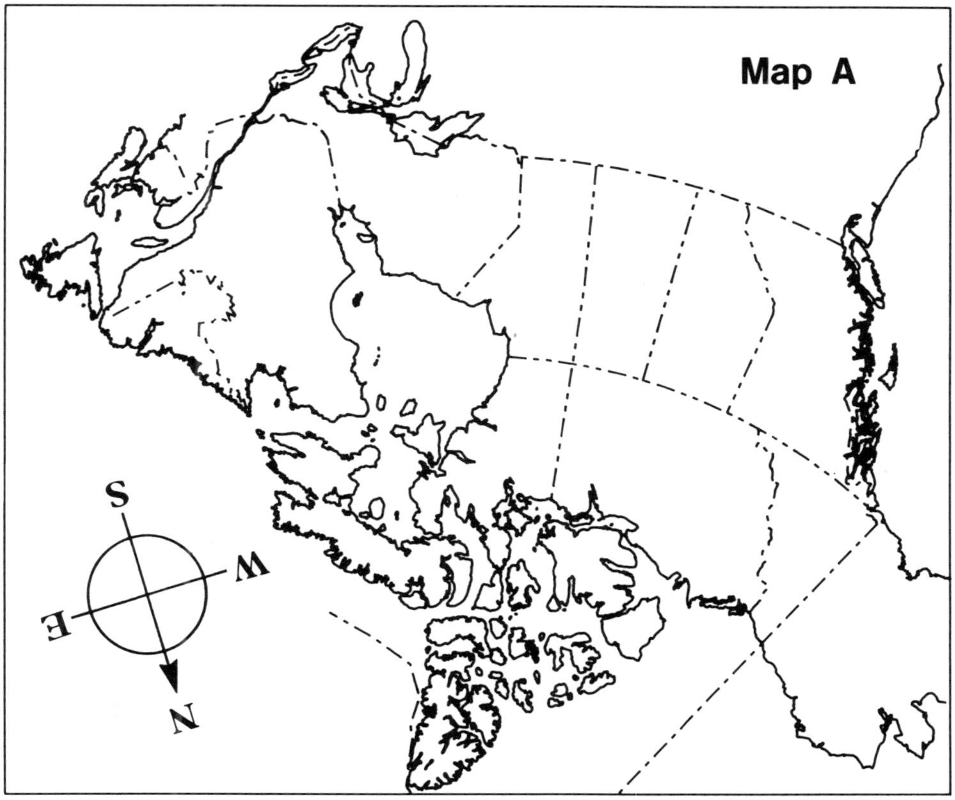

Which map view is incorrect? ________________________

What change would make it correct?

____

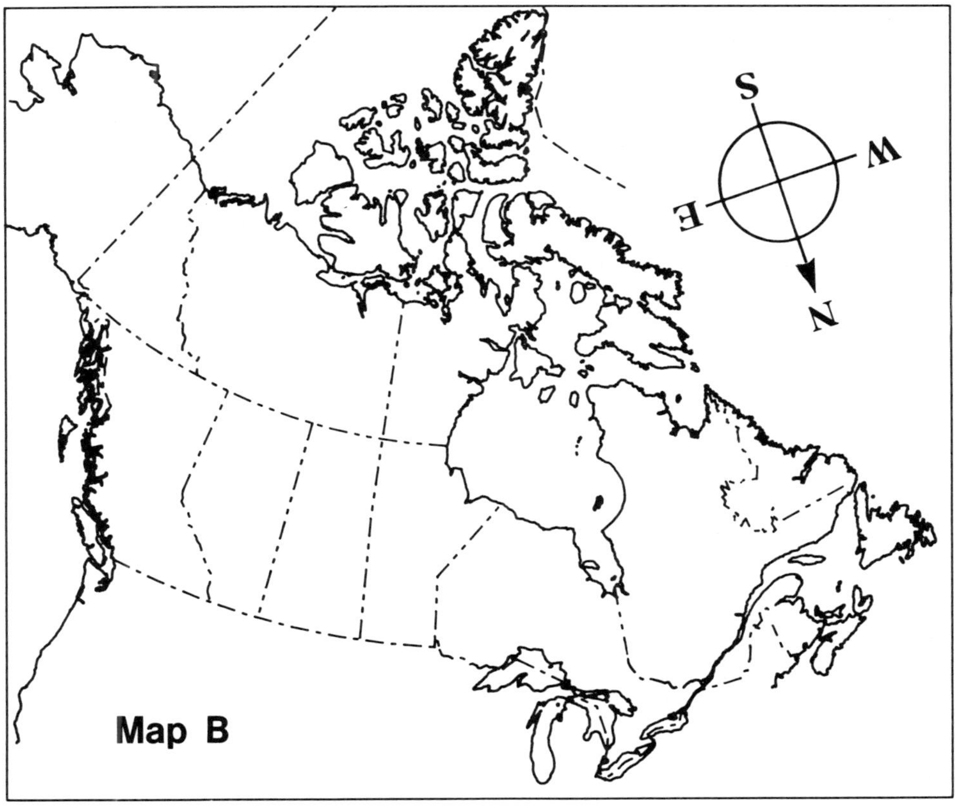

Determining Position on a Map

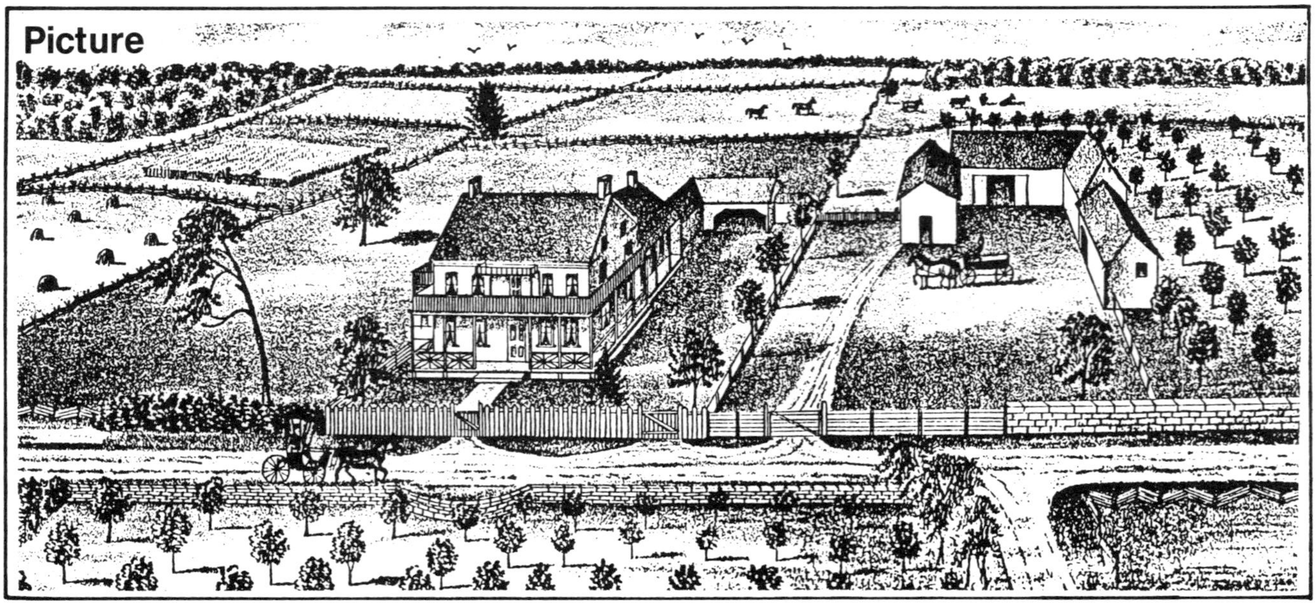

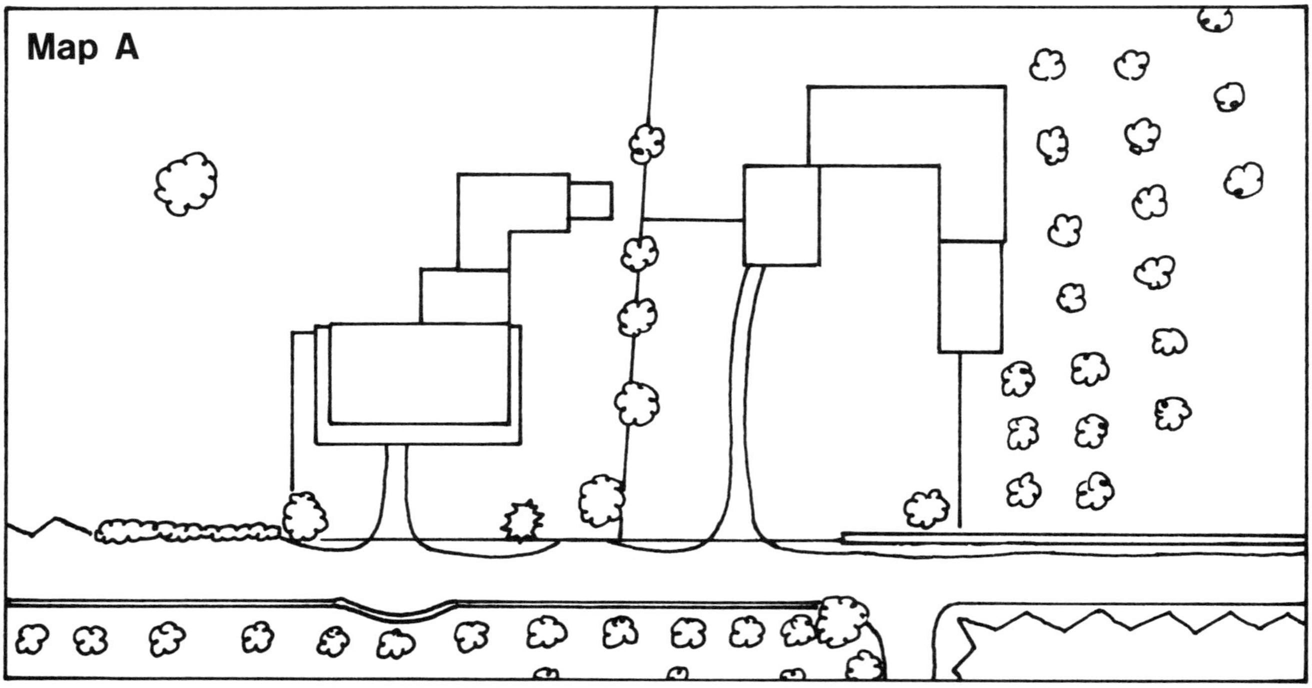

1. In the picture, the farm house is to the (left, right) of the buggy driver.
2. If the buggy driver turns off the road to go into the barn, he will turn (left, right).
3. Put an **X** on Map **A** to show the position of the horse and buggy.
4. Put an **O** on Map **A** to show the position of the wagon and the two horses.
5. Draw a line on Map **A** like this: - - - - - to show the wagon driver's path if he walked from the wagon to the front door of the house.

Using Reference Terms to Describe Position

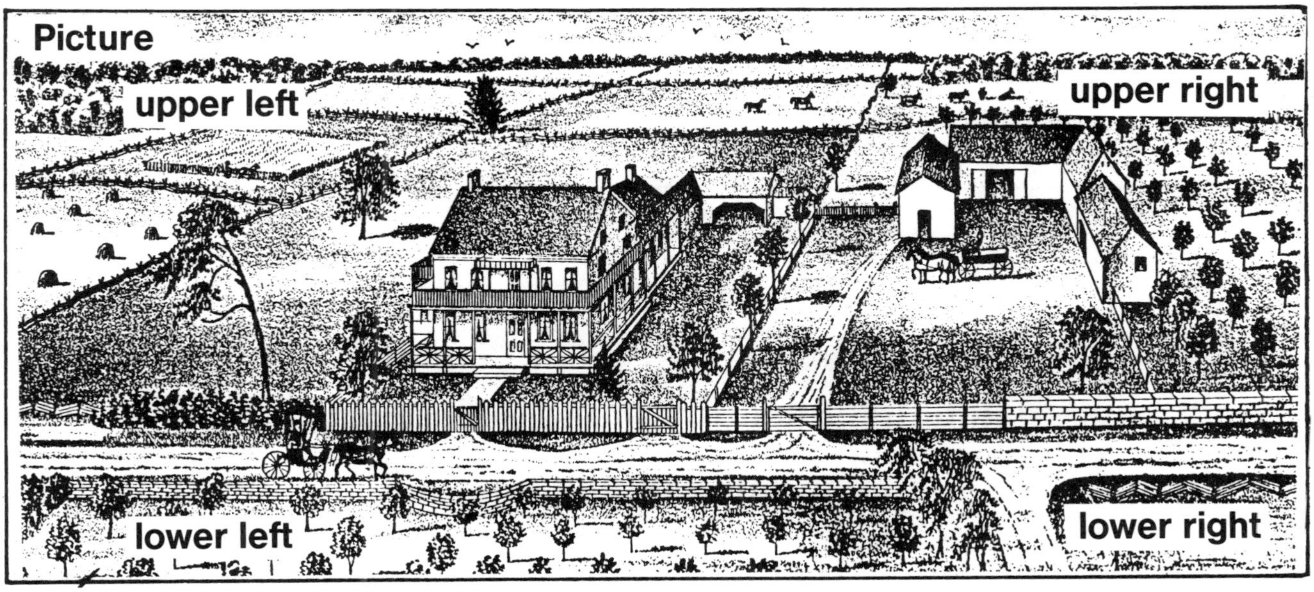

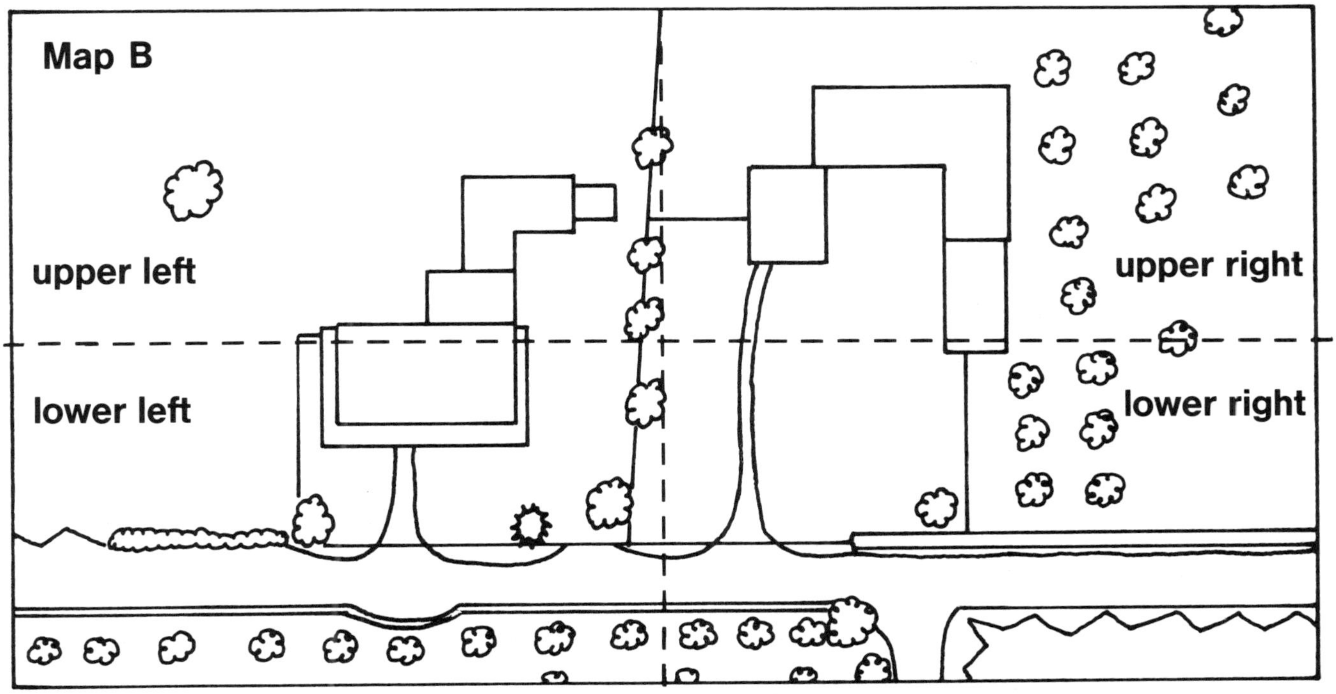

1. Use the picture to identify the building in the lower left part of Map **B**. ______________________
2. In which part of Map **B** is the large barn located? ______________________
3. Which building is nearest the centre of the map? ______________________
4. Describe the position of the wagon and two horses. ______________________
5. It is easier to describe the position of things on Map B than on Map A because

______________________.

Using a Map Grid to Describe Position

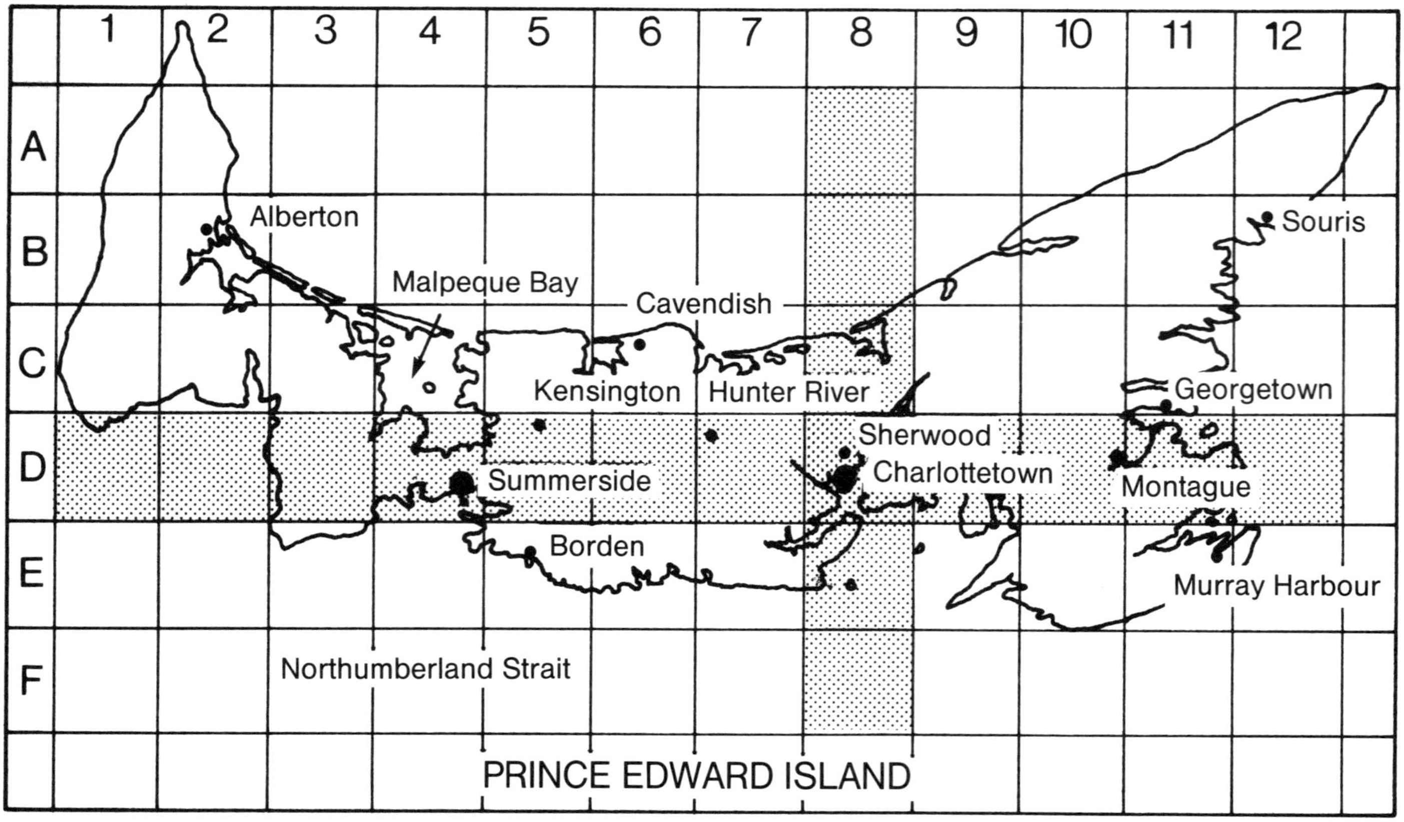

1. The straight lines that cross or intersect on the above map form a network of lines or **grid**.
   The shaded part of the map shows where grid **D** and grid **8** cross each other. This position is called **D8**.
   The **city** in this square or grid is ______________________.

2. The town in **D4** is ______________________.
   b) the town in **E11** is ______________________.
   c) The town in **E5** is ______________________.

3. Use the map grid to describe the position of:
   a) Cavendish – ______
   b) Montague – ______
   c) Hunter River – ______

4. If you live in **E7**, are you closer to Sherwood or Summerside?

   ____

5. Which grid best describes the position of Malpeque Bay?

   ____

Using a Map Grid to Describe Position

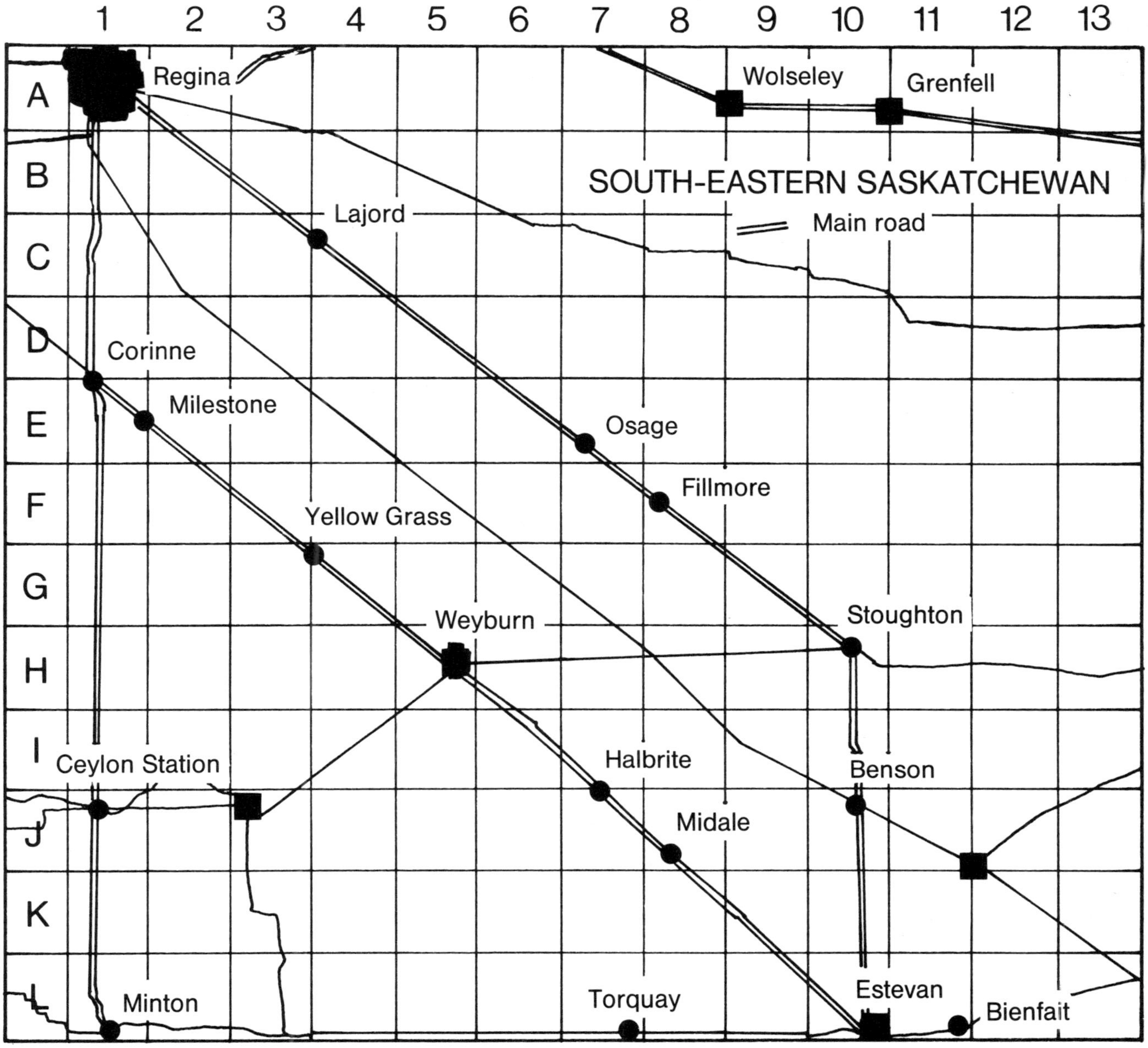

1. The position of the town where grid **E** and grid **7** cross (E7) is

   ________________________.

2. The town in **H5** is ________________________

3. Regina's grid position is ______________

4. Show on the map a good route to take from Estevan to Regina. Stay on the paved roads.

5. List the places you would pass through on your way from Estevan to Regina. Beside each place, state its grid position.

____________________	____________________
____________________	____________________
____________________	____________________
____________________	____________________

Determining Direction by Compass

The compass may have been invented by Arab traders more than 800 years ago. Soon after, Chinese and Viking traders began using a compass to determine north direction. These early compasses were made by carefully placing a metal needle on a little stick of wood so that it floated in a pan of water. The needle was magnetized to point north by rubbing it in one direction across an iron bar.

A compass needle does not point to the geographical North Pole, but to the North Magnetic Pole. The exact position of the North Magnetic Pole was first discovered in 1831. At that time it was near Cape Adelaide in the south-west part of the Boothia Peninsula – the most northern part of the North American mainland. No one knows why, but the position of the North Magnetic Pole changes from year to year. It continues to move slowly north, and in 1980 was located north-west of Bathurst Island.

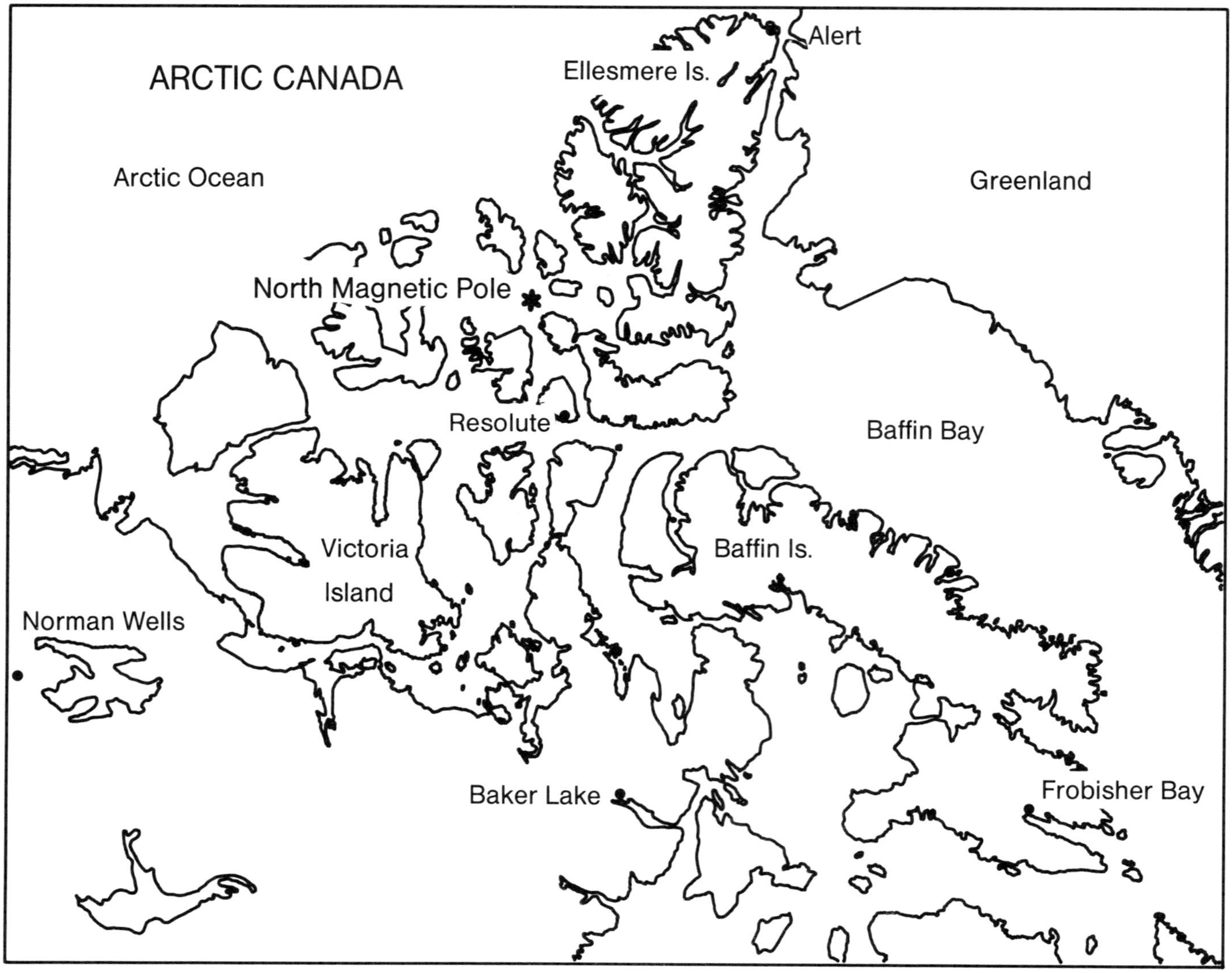

An airplane flies from Frobisher Bay to Resolute. A second plane leaves Baker Lake for Resolute. A third plane flies from Norman Wells to Resolute, and a fourth plane goes from Alert to Resolute. If the pilot in each plane follows a compass for direction, the planes will all **seem** to fly in a north direction. How can this be?

Mystery Bay

Follow the directions to discover the outline of a large body of water in northern Canada that is almost completely surrounded by land. Go only along the edges of the squares or across from corner to corner. Cross each direction off the list as you draw it.

Clue: This bay is named after an English navigator and explorer who discovered it in 1610 while searching for a north-west passage to China.

Begin at **Start.**

1 Go SW 1 space
2 W – 1 space
3 SW – 4
4 S – 3
5 E – 1
6 S – 2
7 SE – 1
8 E – 2
9 SE – 3
10 E – 2
11 S – 3
12 SE – 2
13 NE – 1
14 N – 2
15 NW – 1
16 NE – 2
17 N – 3
18 NW – 1
19 N – 6
20 E – 2

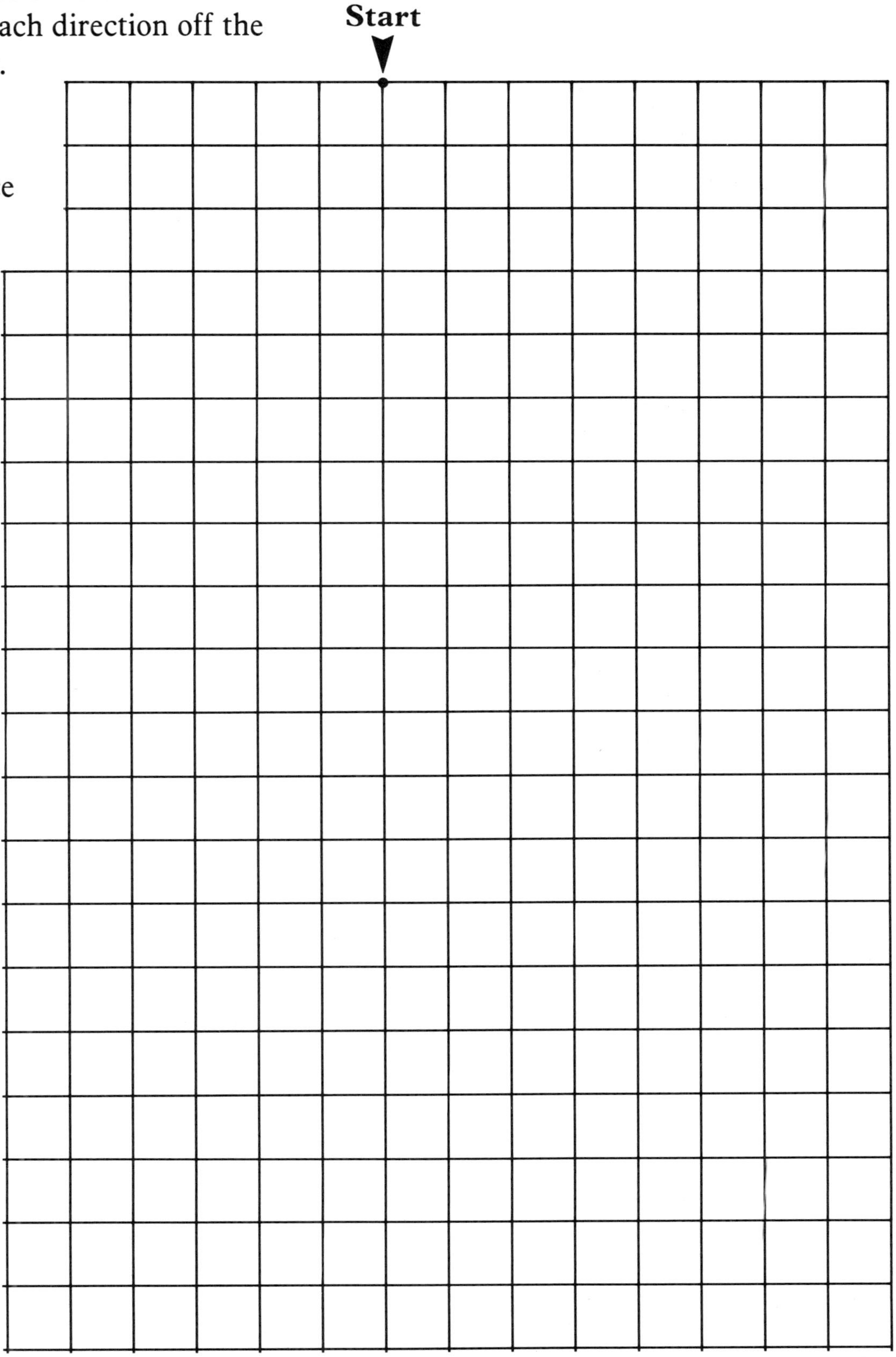

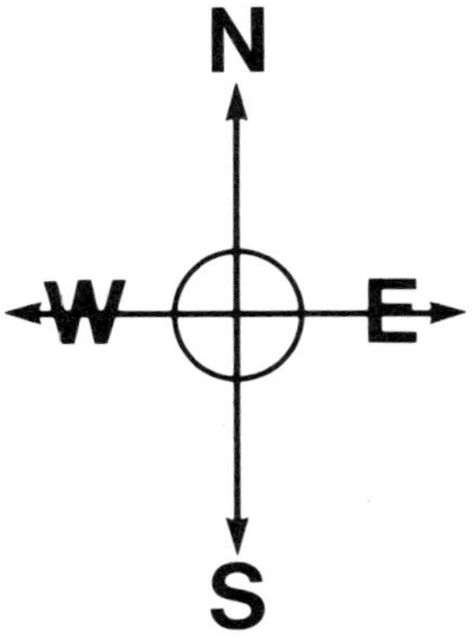

Recognizing Latitude Lines

1. Lines of latitude are imaginary lines that go around the globe in the same east-west direction as the equator. They are like circles, drawn around a ball, that never meet. Which globe shows this, **A** or **B**? ____________

2. Mark the position of the North and South Poles on Globes **A** and **B**.

3. The equator is an imaginary line that divides the earth into two equal parts or hemispheres—northern and southern. The equator is an important line of latitude because from it all other lines of latitude are measured. Show the position of the equator on Globes **A** and **B**.

4. Which line of latitude on the globe is the longest? ____________________

5. Which line of latitude is farthest north? ____________________

   Which line of latitude is farthest south? ____________________

A

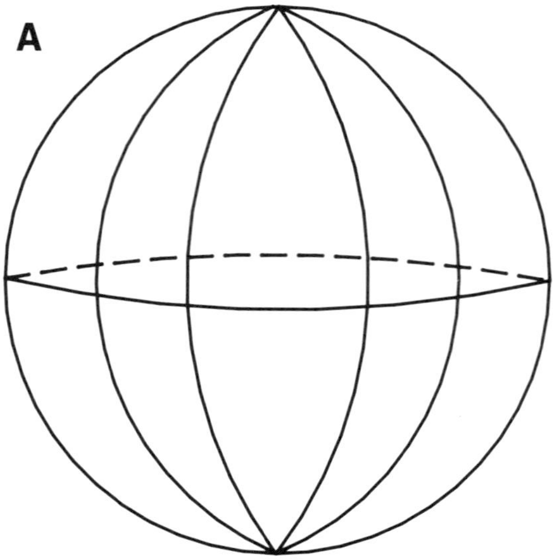

B

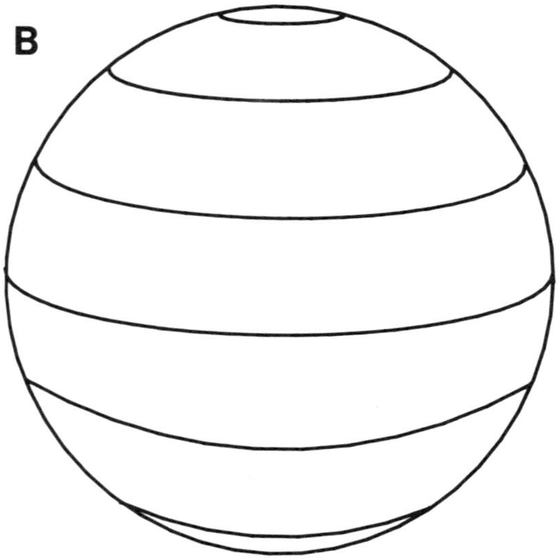

How Latitude is Measured

During the Age of Exploration, new instruments were developed to measure distance and calculate position. Many were not very accurate.

The astrolabe, or "star measurer", had long been used to estimate distance north or south of the equator. From it, the cross-staff was developed. It was used at night to compare the height of certain stars with the horizon and so give the latitude. For day-time readings, the angle between the horizon and the sun's position at noon was measured. The user lined up the three sights on the cross-staff so that the top one pointed directly at the sun, and the bottom one pointed at the horizon. The findings were compared with information in a book on how the earth moved during the year in relation to the sun and the stars. However, a cross-staff could not be used when it was often needed most—during cloudy or stormy weather.

A sextant works in almost the same way. To-day, navigators on ships and planes use an automatic sextant to record their position.

Using Latitude to Find Position

Latitude lines, or parallels of latitude, are imaginary lines running east-west around the earth. They are like parallel circles drawn around the globe and are measured in degrees **north** or **south** of the equator. The equator is 0 degrees.

If a globe is unrolled into a map, the lines of latitude might look like the lines on this map. Notice that the distances at the North and South Poles seem to be as wide as the equator. On this kind of map, only the north-south distances are correct.

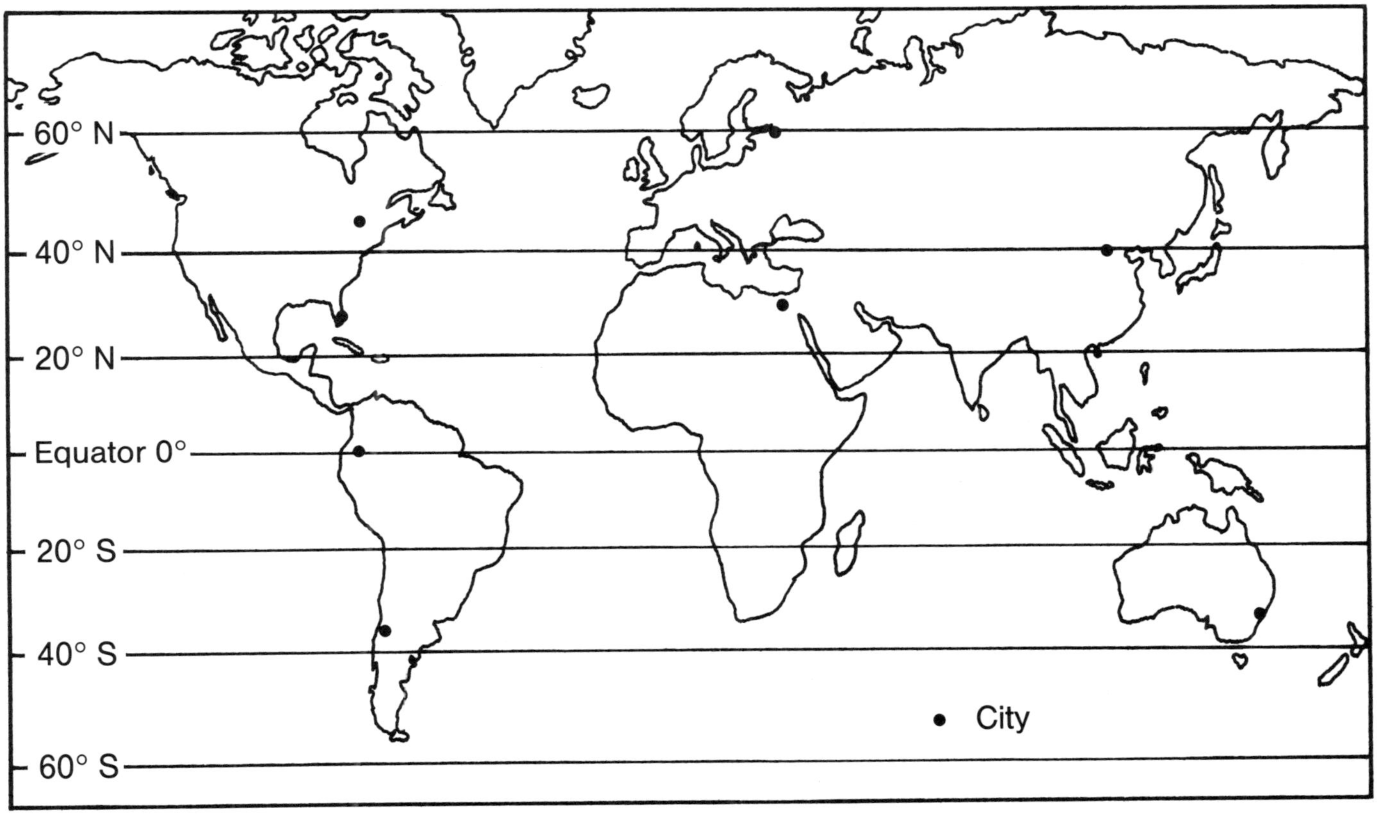

1. These eight cities are at different latitudes. Put the name of each city in its correct place on the map.

   Cairo, Egypt – 30° North
   Leningrad, U.S.S.R. – 60° N
   Miami, U.S.A. – 25° N
   Ottawa, Canada – 45° N
   Peking, China – 40° N
   Quito, Ecuador – 0°
   Santiago, Chile – 35° S
   Sydney, Australia – 34° S

2. The city nearest the equator is

   ____________________.

3. The city farthest north is

   ____________________.

4. The city closest to the South Pole is

   ____________________.

5. The two cities that are at almost the same latitude are

   ____________________ and

   ____________________.

Recognizing Longitude Lines

The equator divides the globe into two halves—northern and southern hemispheres. Another line also divides the globe into two equal parts or hemispheres—eastern and western. This line of longitude is called the Prime Meridian. Prime means first or beginning.

All other lines of longitude are measured in degrees east or west of the Prime Meridian. Lines of longitude are like half-circles drawn around the globe that come together at the North and South Poles.

A

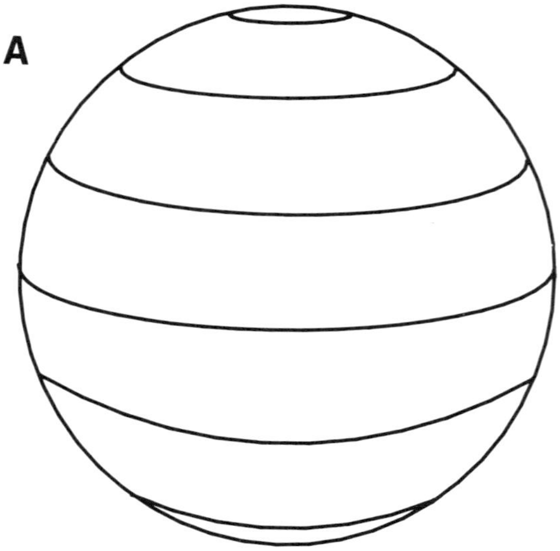

B

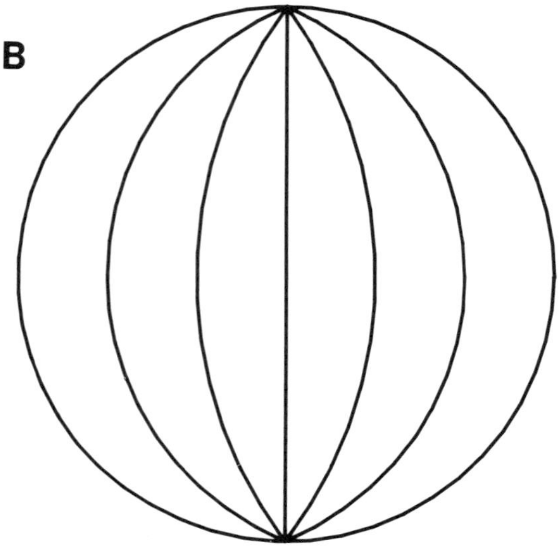

1. Which globe shows this, A or B?
2. Which globe shows the position of the Prime Meridian? ____________
3. Lines of longitude are also called

______________________________.

The Origin of the Prime Meridian

As new lands and oceans were discovered, it became more important for explorers to know their exact position. Navigators had found ways to determine their position north or south of the equator. However, they had difficulty establishing lines from which to measure east-west distances. They needed these lines to give them a cross-reference for charting their position and course more accurately. Different countries established longitude lines to measure east-west distance, but could not agree on a common point to begin their measurement.

Finally, in 1759, an English inventor named John Harrison developed the marine chronometer. This instrument gave ship's navigators the exact time from which to calculate their position east or west of a certain point. Because his laboratory was in Greenwich, at that time a suburb of London, a base line was drawn to pass through Greenwich, England. The exact spot marking of this Prime Meridian was a brass strip set in paving and was marked zero degrees longitude.

Since 1884, most countries have agreed to measure time from this line of longitude. To-day, the world's time zones are based on Greenwich Mean (or Standard) Time. The time is kept accurate by six atomic clocks that lose no more than one second each 4000 years! From its radio signals, ships and other moving objects around the world can check their exact east-west position.

Using Longitude to Find Position

A globe can be divided into segments or degrees. These segments, or lines of longitude, are used to measure distance **east** or **west** of the Prime Meridian. The Prime Meridian is an imaginary line, marked 0 degrees, that passes both geographical poles through Greenwich, England.

1. If a globe is unrolled into a map, the lines of longitude might look like those on this map. In what way are the longitude lines on this map different from those on a globe?

____

______________________________________.

2. Show on the map the position of the Prime Meridian.

3. These eight cities are at various lines of longitude. Put the name of each city in its correct place on the map.

Adelaide, Australia – 140° East
London, England – 0°
Miami, U.S.A. – 80° W
Madras, India – 80° E
Ottawa, Canada – 75° W
Santiago, Chile – 70° W
Tokyo, Japan – 140° E
Vancouver, B.C. – 123° W

4. The city located on the Prime Meridian is ______________________.

5. The city farthest west of the Prime Meridian is ______________________.

6. The two cities that are on the same longitude line are

______________________ and

______________________.

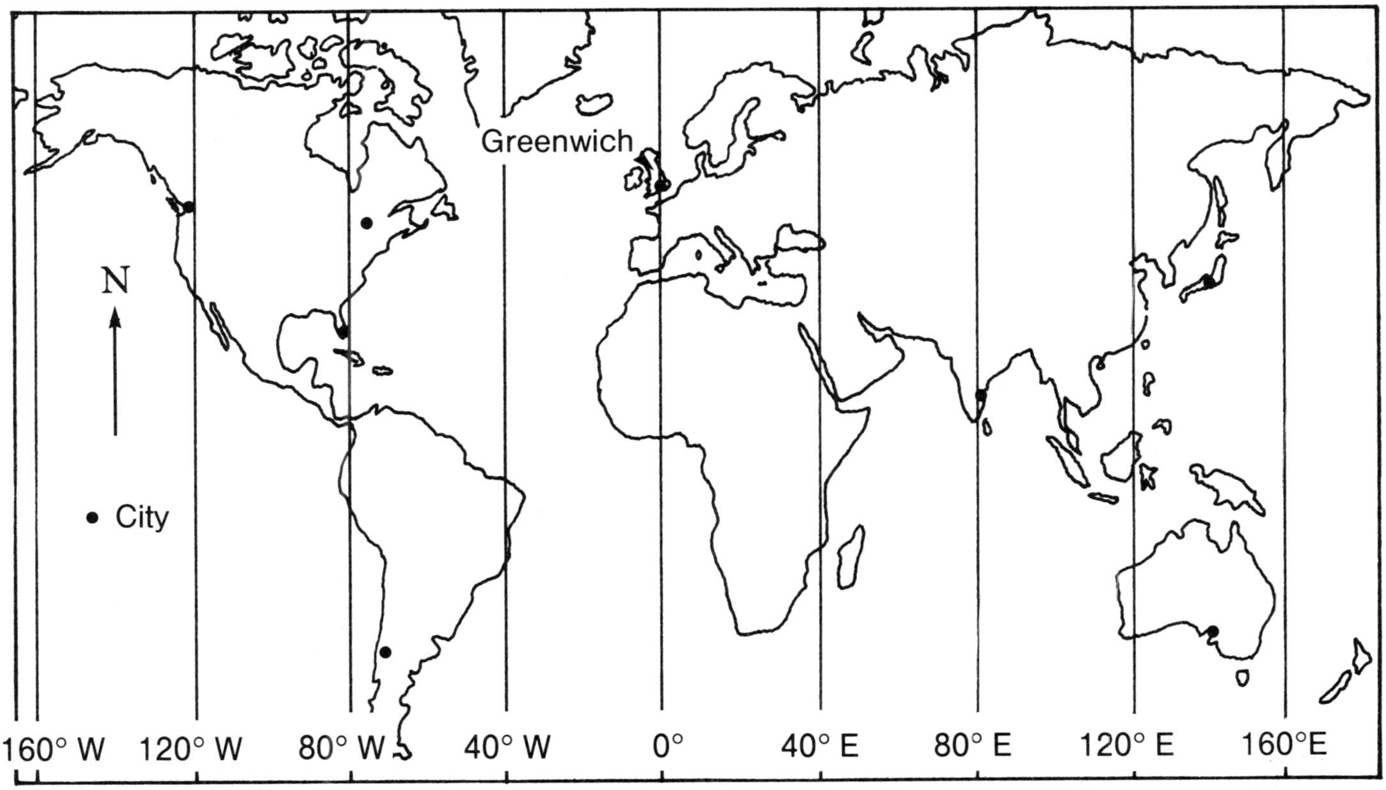

Using a Map Grid to Determine Position

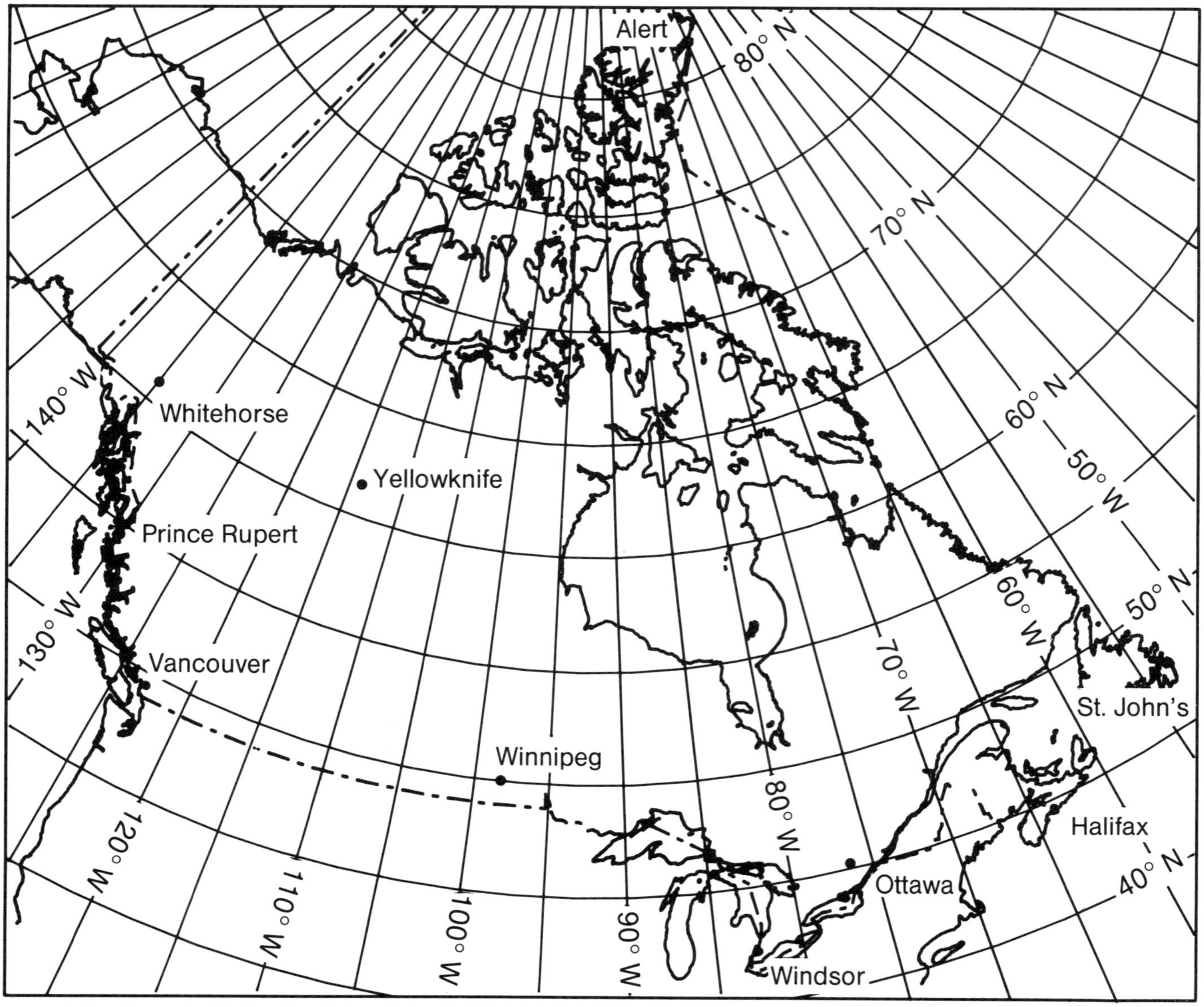

Latitude lines give the position of a place in degrees north or south of the equator. Longitude lines give the position of a place in degrees east or west of the Prime Meridian.

When lines of latitude and lines of longitude are placed together, they form a network of lines or grid. Using such a map grid, it is possible to find the position of any place on the earth's surface. On some map projections, the grid lines are curved like the earth's surface, for greater accuracy.

Use the map grid to complete this chart:

Place		Latitude	Longitude
________________	1	83° N	63° W
Halifax	2	_____	63° W
Ottawa	3	_____	_____
Prince Rupert	4	54° N	_____
________________	5	48° N	53° W
Vancouver	6	_____	123° w
________________	7	62° N	114° W
________________	8	61° N	135° W
________________	9	42° N	83° W
Winnipeg	10	_____	97° W

Identifying Position

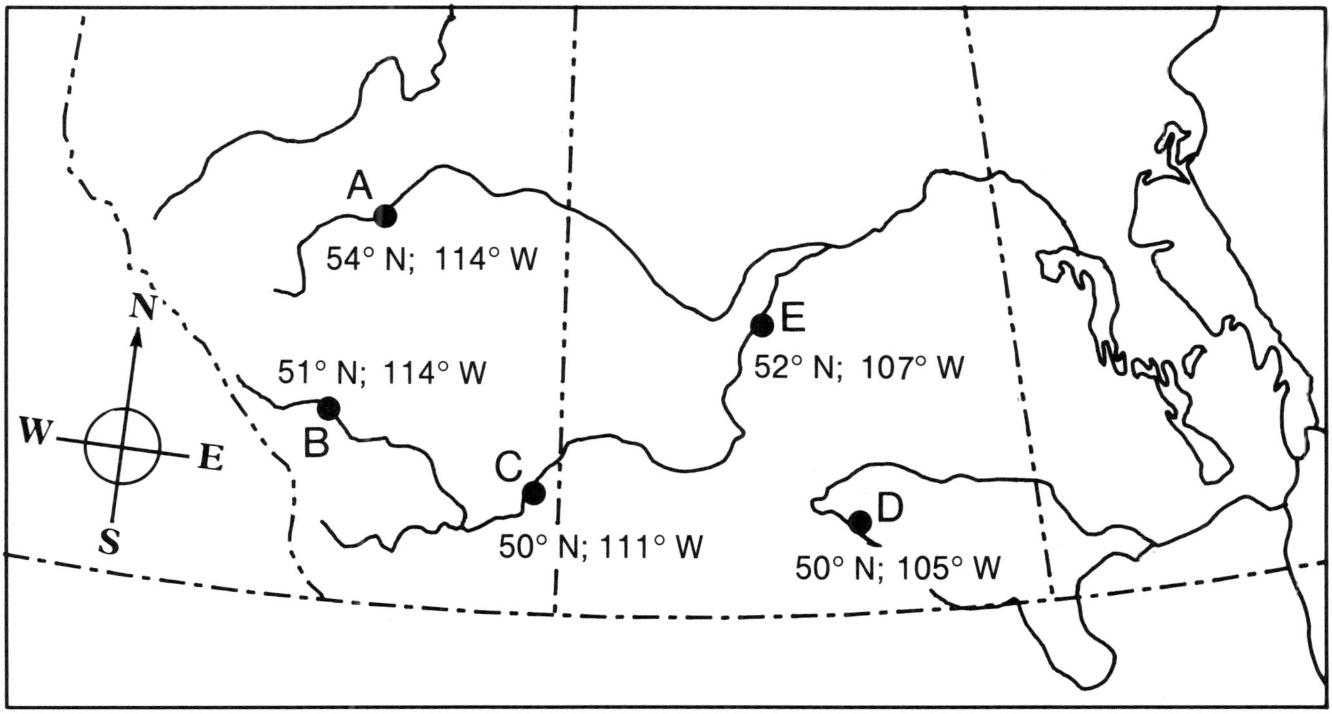

1. The map shows the position of five prairie towns or cities. Use an atlas to help you find the name of each place. Print the correct name beside each letter.
2. Complete each sentence by writing the direction more accurately.
   a) Place **A** is north-______________ of place **D**.
   b) **D** is south-______________ of **E**.
   c) **C** is south-______________ of **E**.
   d) **E** is north-______________ of **C**.
3. You are a pilot. The six Canadian cities on your flight path are summarized below as reference points. Name each city. Use an atlas to help you.

   You leave from a) 49° N; 123° W (______________________).

Your plane lands at b) 51° N; 114° W (______________________) to take on mail.

Then you fly on to c) 50° N; 105° W (______________________) to refuel and take on more mail. You fly over d) 50° N; 97° W (______________________) on your way to e) 44° N; 79° W (______________________), which is the end of your flight.

4. In which two main directions was the aircraft travelling as it flew from place (a) to place (e)?

   ______________________ and ______________________

Canada Crossword

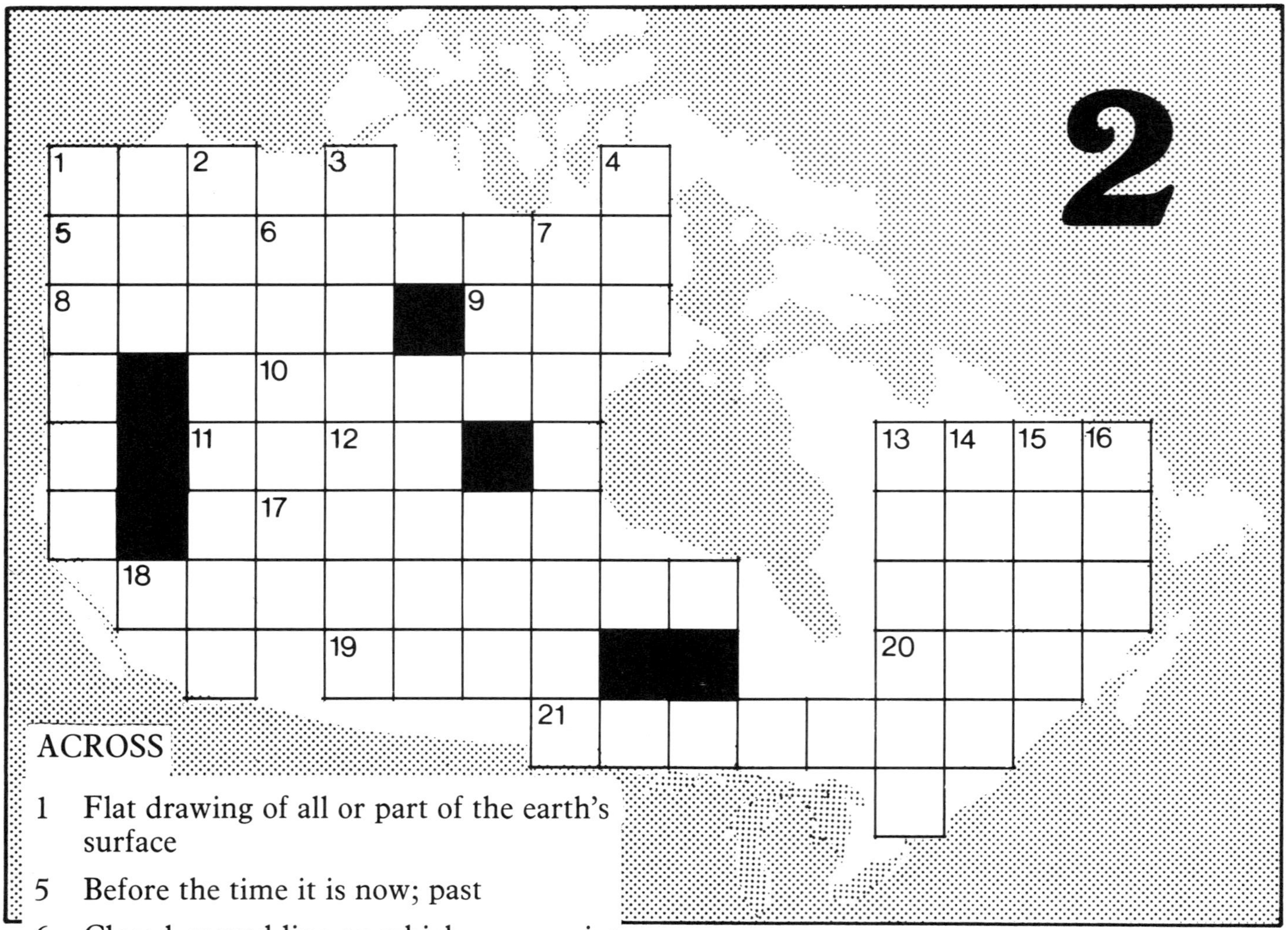

ACROSS

1 Flat drawing of all or part of the earth's surface

5 Before the time it is now; past

6 Closed curved line on which every point is the same distance from the centre point

8 A sudden, heavy flow, to pour out suddenly

9 Part of a sea or lake that stretches into the land

10 Firm, secure

11 A long, hollow pipe

13 One of two equal parts

17 Correct or true, opposite of left

18 Distance east or west on the earth's surface, measured in degrees

19 System of survey lines running parallel to lines of latitude and longitude

20 To place, put in some place

21 Imaginary circle around the earth, halfway between the North Pole and the South Pole

DOWN

1 Stone or piece of metal that attracts iron or steel

2 Place where a person or thing is

3 The end part or point

4 Piece of metal used to open a lock

7 Distance north or south of the equator, measured in degrees

10 Rotate, move around as a wheel does

12 Large, great in size or amount

13 Large bay in Canada, named after an early English explorer

14 Behind, later

15 Opposite of right

16 A long way, at a great distance, not near

Interpreting Symbols

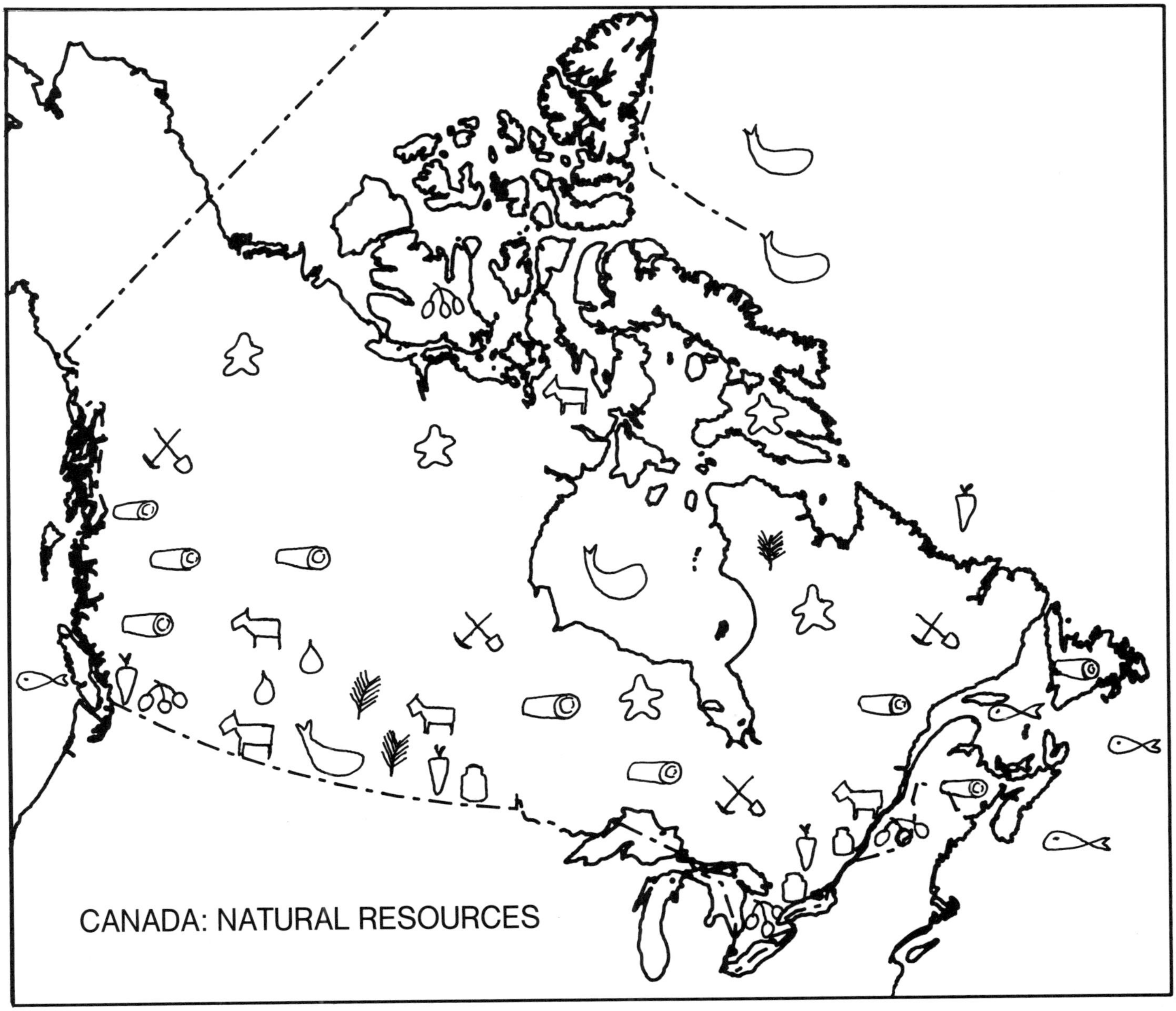

Beef cattle	Fishing
Dairy cattle	Furs
Fruit	Minerals
Grains	Oil
Vegetables	Wood (timber)
	Whaling and sealing

Find and circle the five symbols on this map that are shown in the wrong place.

Identifying Map Symbols

Maps are made up of small drawings called symbols. A symbol **represents** or stands for an idea or thing in simplified form. Map symbols are like carefully chosen words of a message, because some symbols are more important than others. If you understand the meaning of the symbols, you can read the map as easily as you would read a telegram or message.

1. What does this symbol represent or show?

____

2. These symbols on different maps might also represent

_____________________.

3. Draw a symbol to represent high mountains.

4. Draw a symbol to represent low hills.

5. Pick out five different symbols that are shown on this map. Beside each symbol, write what you think it represents.

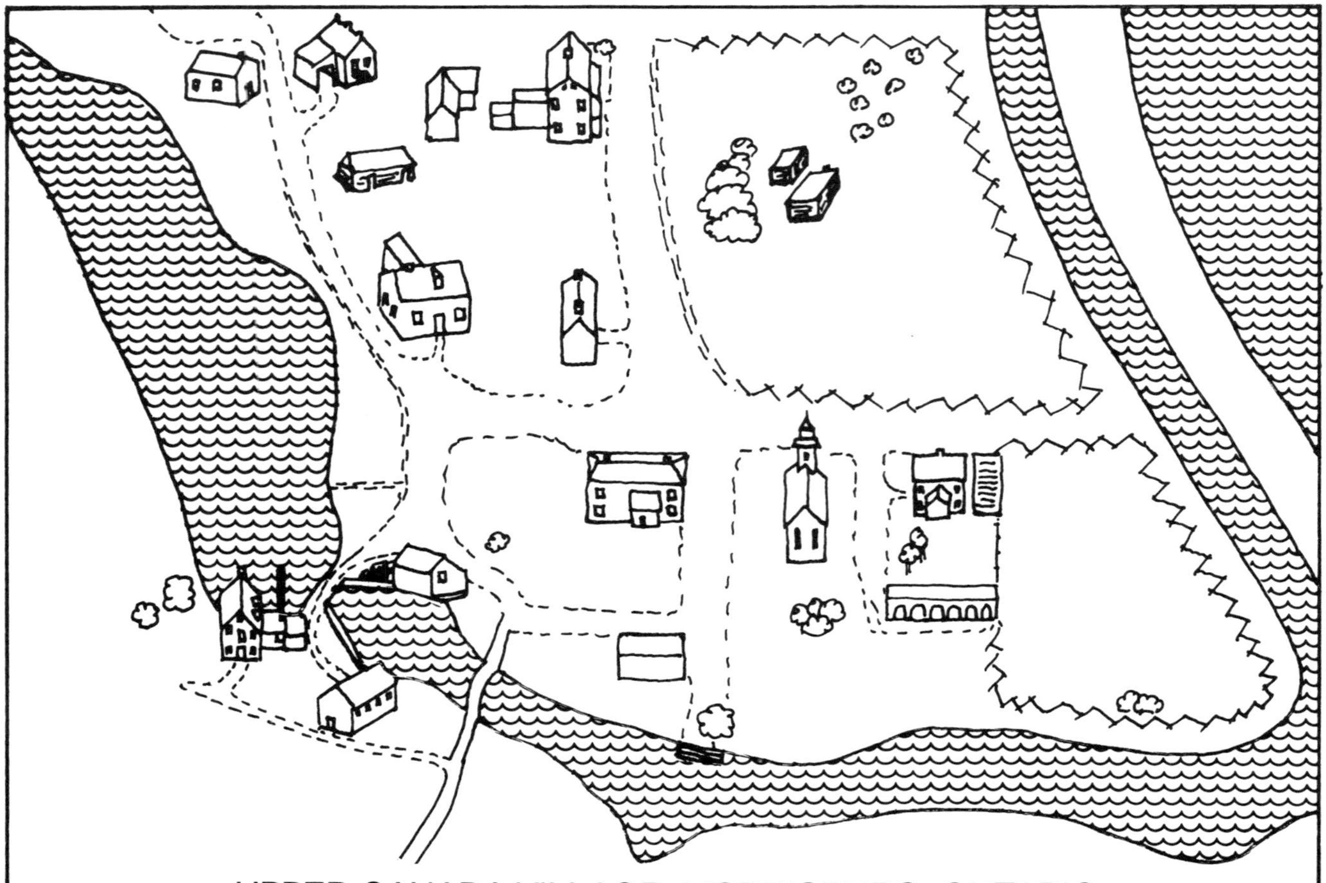

UPPER CANADA VILLAGE, MORRISBURG, ONTARIO

Map Puzzle

The symbols in this early map-picture tell a story. In 1619, a Dutch explorer, Captain Jens Munck and his crew, were caught unprepared at the mouth of the Churchill River by an early winter. In order to survive the cold ahead, they quickly had to do a number of things. Can you identify at least three?

1 ____

2 ____

3 ____

Reading a Map Legend

1. Map **A** is easier to read than Map **B** because ______________________

____

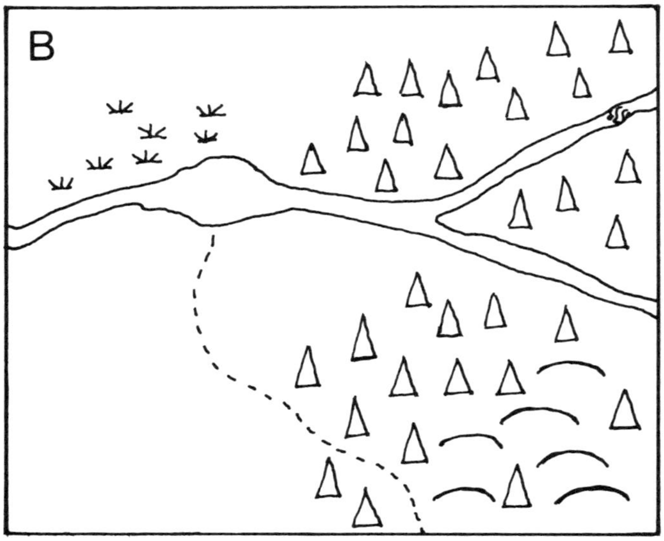

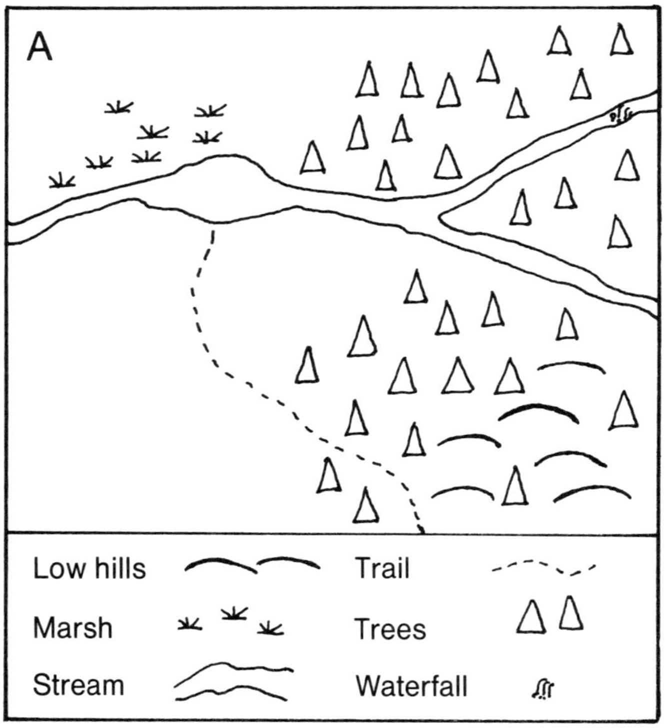

2. A map legend explains the meaning of the important symbols on the map. Another term for map legend is map **key.** Why is this a good term?

____

3. Most map legends do not include every symbol that is on the map. Often-used symbols do not have to be explained each time they are shown. These symbols are not usually included in a legend:

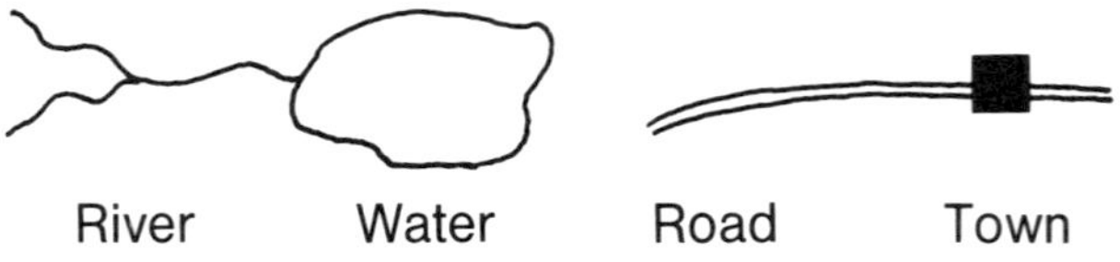

List some other symbols that you think might not be included in a map legend.

____

____

4. A symbol should look like, or suggest the feature it stands for. Why is Map **C** difficult to read?

____

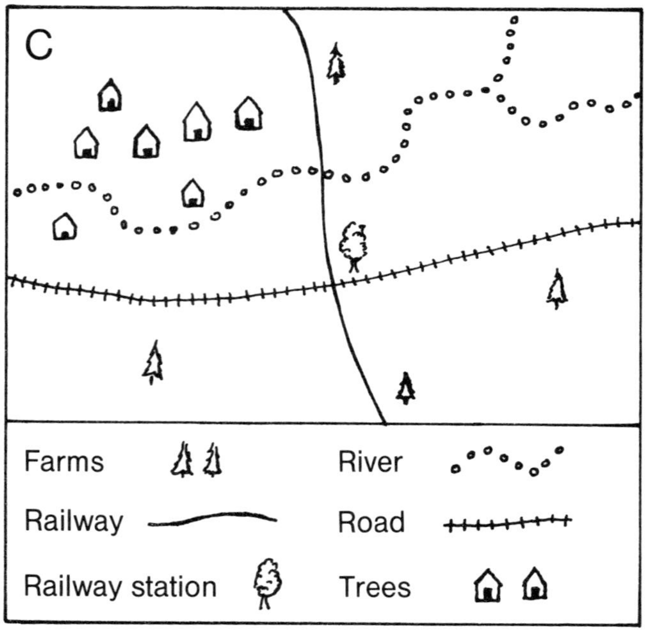

What should you remember when you make up map symbols?

____

Identifying Physical and Cultural Symbols

Map symbols can be divided into two groups:
nature-made or natural — river, swamp
people-made or cultural — road, building

Natural Symbols	Cultural Symbols

1. Decide where to place the following words in the above chart.

   island
   town
   airport
   hill
   gold-mine
   fence
   orchard
   barn
   hospital
   forest
   beach
   waterfall

2. Use the legend to underline the natural symbols shown on Map **A**.

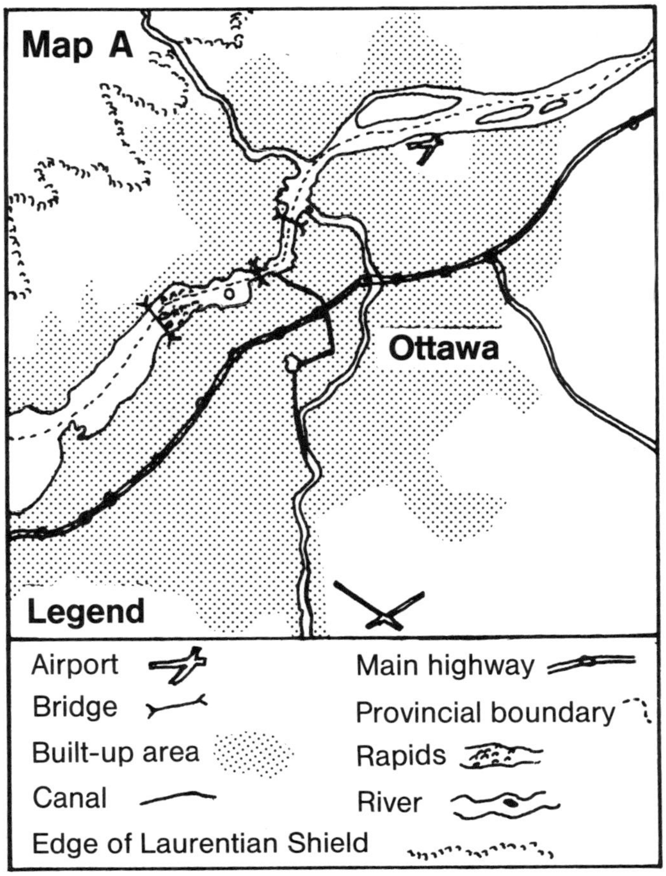

3. The legend on Map **B** shows four **natural** symbols. Draw at least four **cultural** symbols on this map. Remember to explain your symbols in the legend.

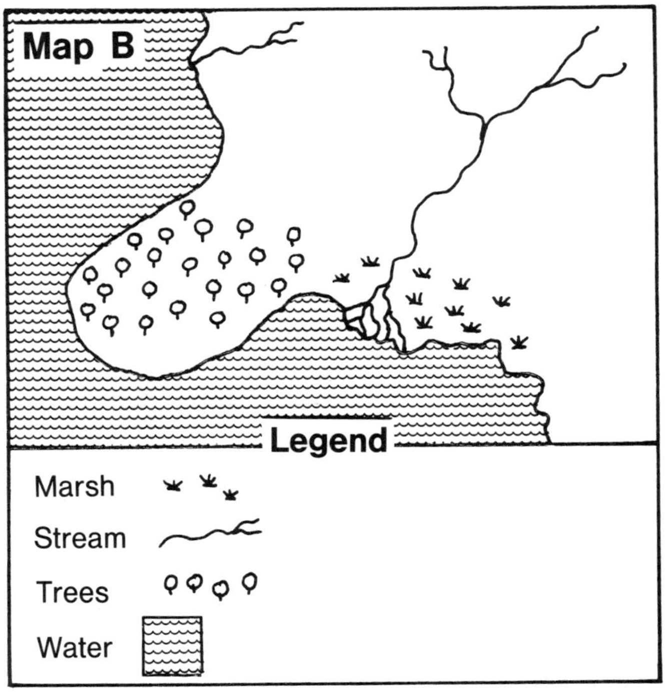

Interpreting Point and Line Symbols

Many maps contain line symbols. Some lines represent natural routes, such as rivers. Other lines represent "people-made" routes, such as roads or highways.

Maps can also include point symbols. The most common points represent cities and towns. Can you find another point symbol on this map?

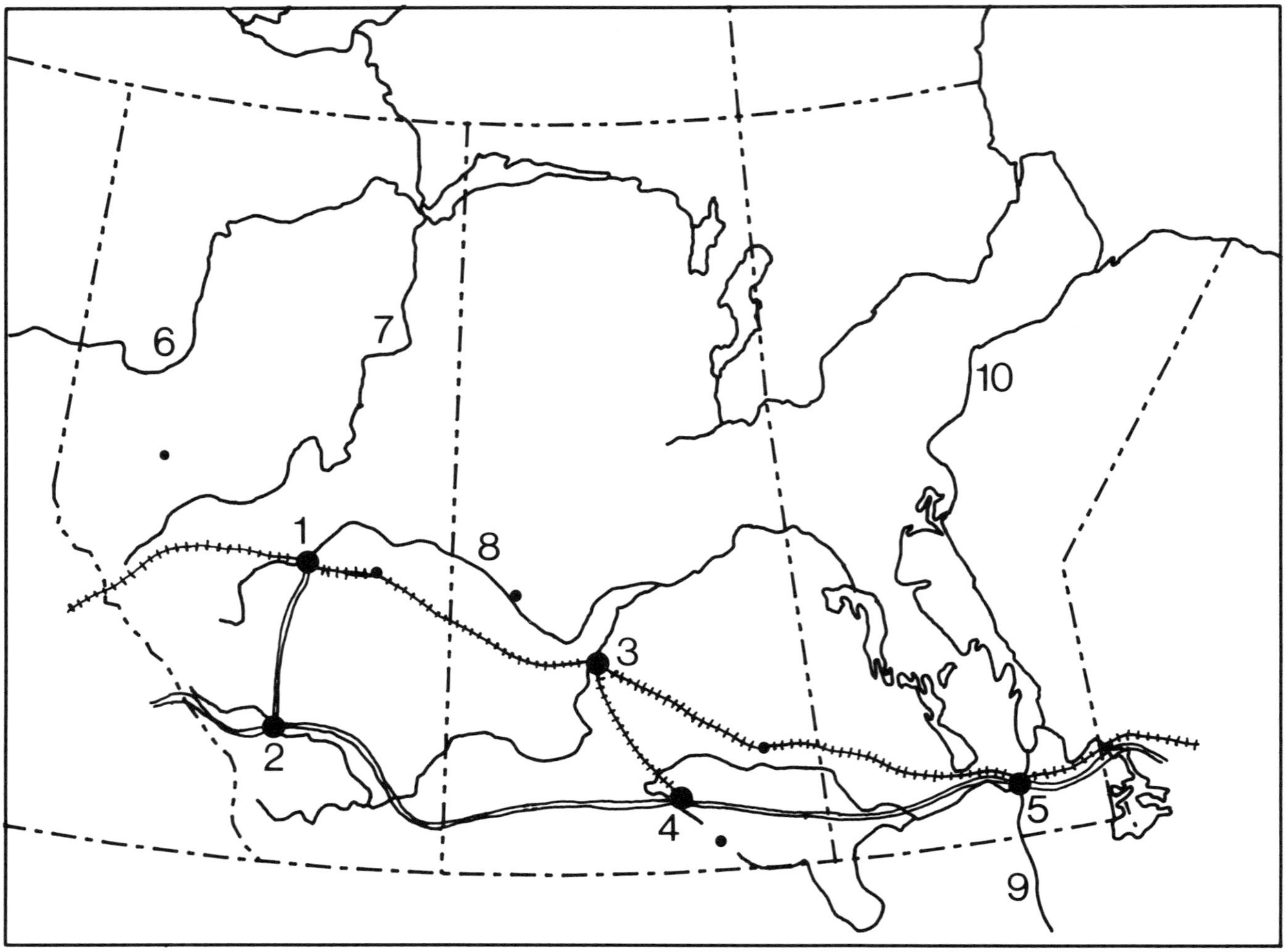

Legend

River

Main highway

Railway

City

Town

Provincial boundary

1. Complete the map legend to show the meaning of the different lines and points.
2. Name the three provinces shown on the map.

____

____

____

3. On the map, name the **cities** represented by points 1 to 5.
4. On the map, name the **rivers** represented by lines 6 to 10.
5. Give this map a suitable title.

____

Interpreting Shading Symbols

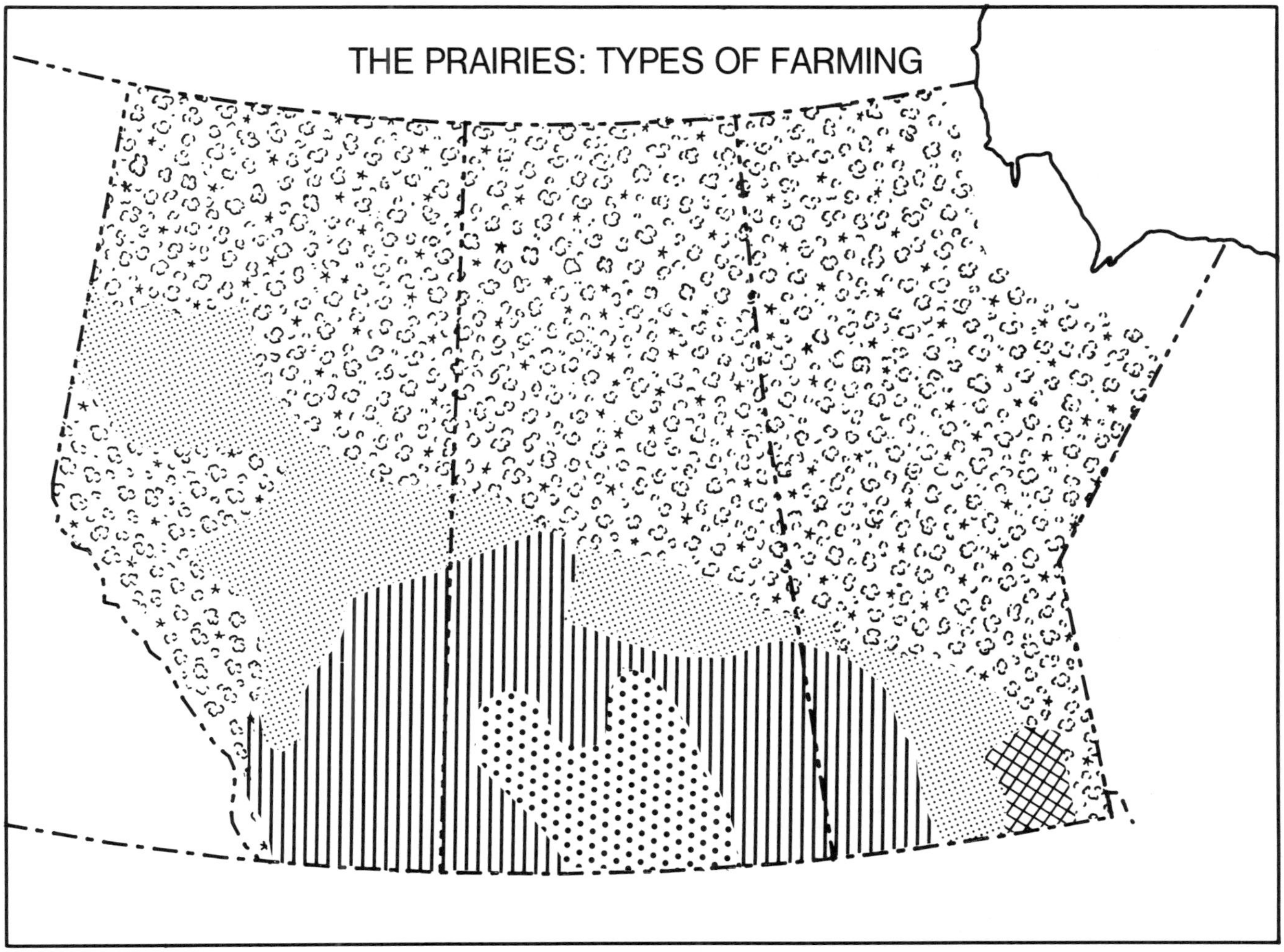

Legend

- Wheat
- Cattle-grain
- Grain-mixed livestock
- Mixed livestock-dairy cattle
- Forest

1. Which symbol shows wheat farming?

____

2. Which province has the largest area in wheat?

____

3. Name two kinds of farming that are found in all three provinces.

____

4. Which province has the largest area in cattle and grain?

____

5. What is the land used for in the northern part of each province?

____

Using Contours to Show Height

1. Mark these things on the **picture**:
   mountains
   mountain peak
   slope
   valley
   river
   lake
   flat lowland
   ocean (sea level)
2. Mark the highest point in the picture with an **"H"**.
3. Mark the lowest point with an **"L"**.

GREATER VANCOUVER REGION

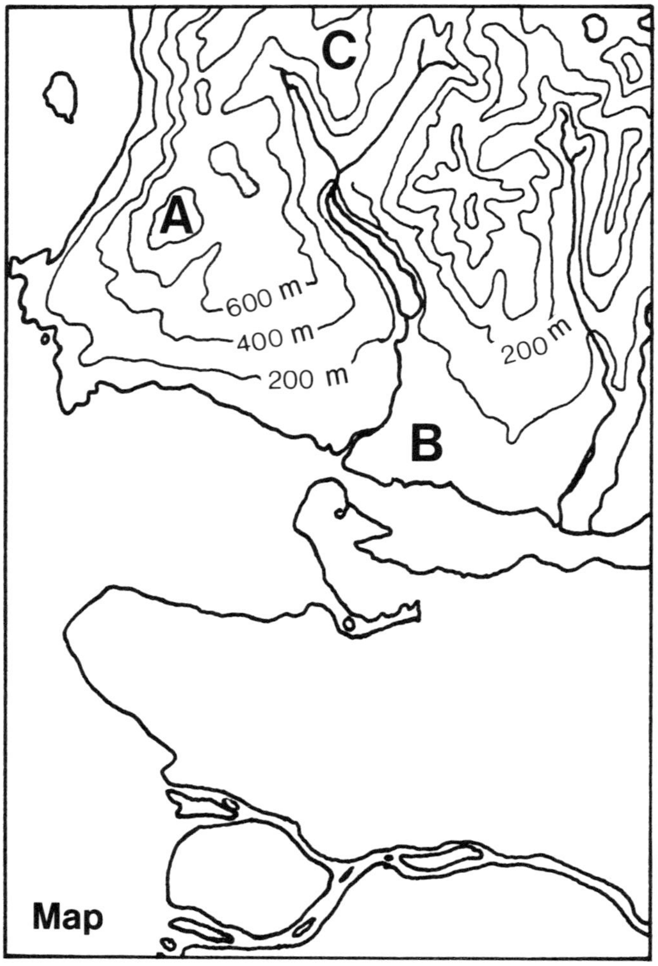

4. This is a map of the same area. On this map, numbered lines, called **contours** show height. What do the numbers on some of the lines mean?

   ______________________________.

5. Mark these things on the **map**:
   mountain peak
   slope
   valley
   river
   lake
   flat lowland
   ocean (sea level)
6. Which point on the map is highest, **A, B, or C?**

   ______________________________.

Using Colour to Show Height

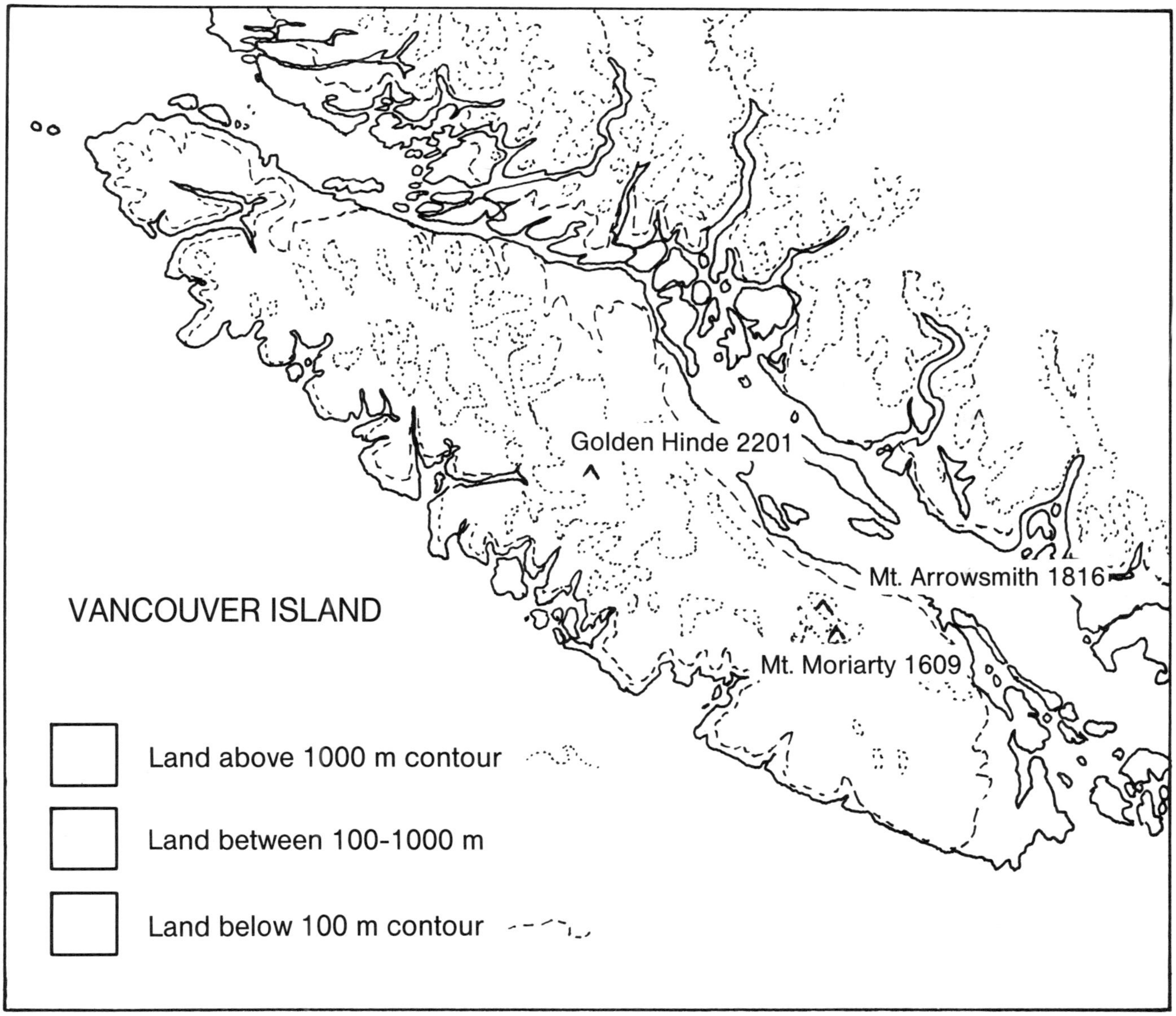

1. Colour the land below the 100 metre contour line green.
2. Colour the land above the 1000 metre contour line brown.
3. Shade in the land in between in yellow. Remember to complete the map legend to explain your colour choice.
4. What do the three sets of numbers on the map mean?

   ____.

5. Where is the highest elevation on Vancouver Island?

   ____.

Interpreting Symbols on an Early Map

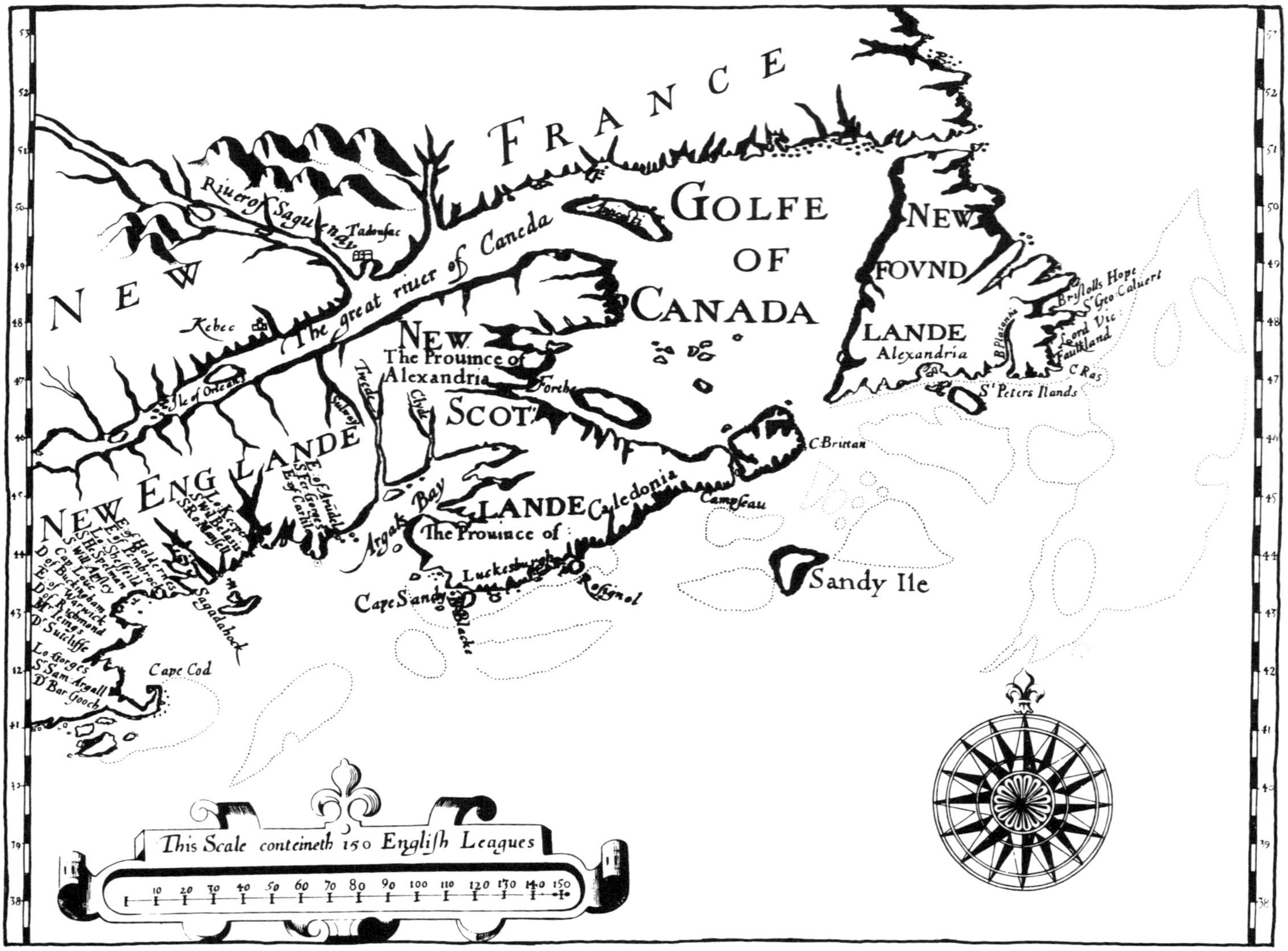

1. This early map of Canada was made in 1624.
   Which part of Canada is shown?

   ____

2. How can you tell that this is an old map?

   ____

   ____

   ____

   ____

   ____

3. Use an atlas or another map of Canada to find the present name of these places:
   - The great river of Canada
   - Sandy Isle
   - Argals Bay
   - Kebec
   - New France
   - New Scot Lande

4. Draw the symbols that are used in this map which show:
   - hills
   - rivers
   - islands
   - shallow water (fishing banks)
   - French towns (forts)

Map Puzzle

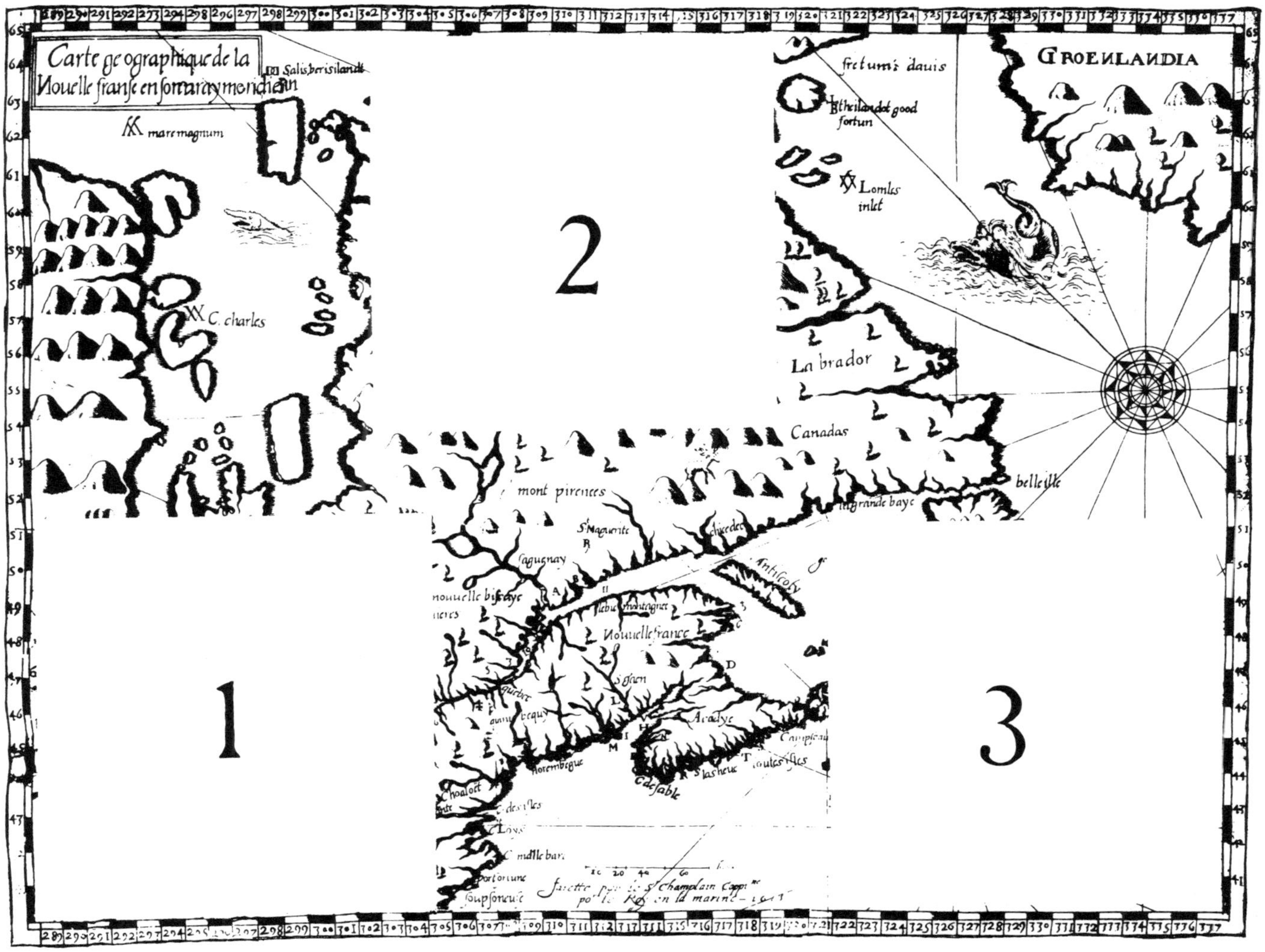

Cut out the squares below; then fit each square in its proper place in the above frame. When complete, you will have a copy of an early map made in 1619 by Samuel de Champlain. Which part of Canada does the map show?

____

A

B

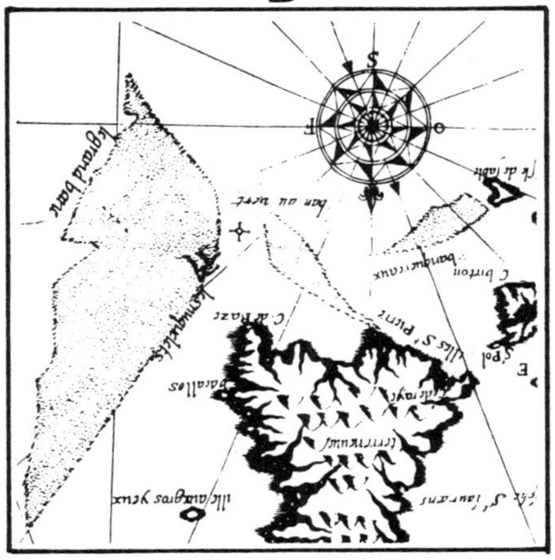

C

Relating Text Information to a Map

Sir Alexander Mackenzie was a fur-trader and explorer who made two great exploration journeys into north-western Canada. Both times, he was searching for a water route between the Atlantic and Pacific Oceans.

Mackenzie's first journey took him to the Arctic Ocean. In June, 1789, he left Fort Chipewyan on Lake Athabaska. He and his guides paddled by canoe down the Slave River to Great Slave Lake and down a large river that Mackenzie later named after himself. He reached the shores of the Arctic Ocean in mid-July.

Four years later, Mackenzie travelled west. Leaving Lake Athabaska in May, 1793, he paddled up the Peace River. He crossed the mountains by way of the Parsnip and Fraser Rivers, and continued down the Bella Coola River to the tidewater of the Pacific Ocean.

Alexander Mackenzie was the first recorded person to cross what is now Canada by land. He also proved through these two explorations that no navigable water route existed from the Pacific to the Arctic through the continent.

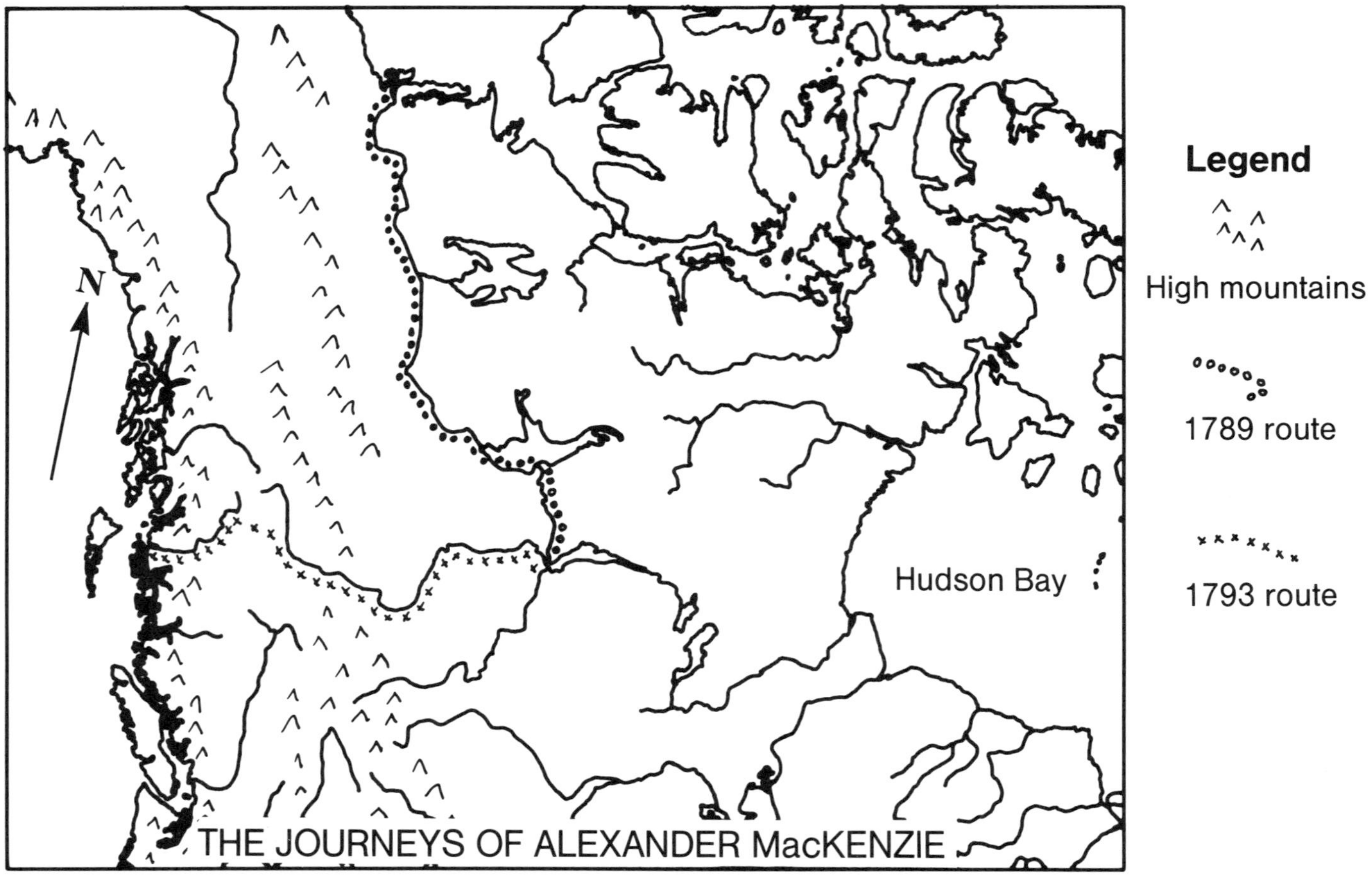

1. From which large lake did Mackenzie begin both journeys? Mark it on the map.
2. What is the meaning of this line on the map? °°°°°°°°
3. What is the meaning of this line on the map? ××××××××
4. In his 1789 travels, Mackenzie discovered a great river. Print the name of this river on the map. Name the ocean that it empties into.
5. In which main direction did Mackenzie travel on his second journey? Name the large mountain ranges that he crossed.

Interpreting Symbols on Different Maps

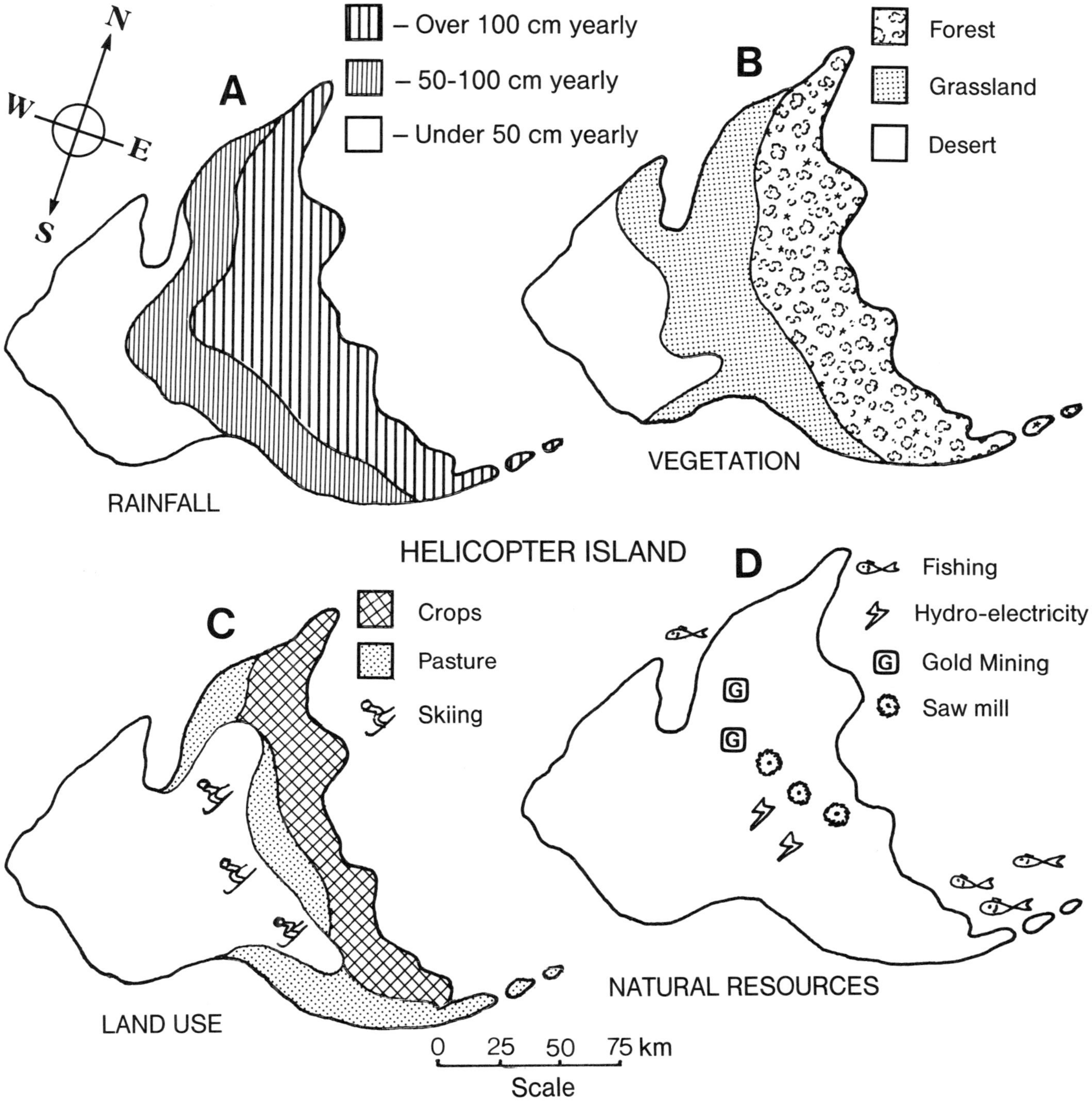

1. Above, are four different maps of an imaginary island. Use the legend beside each map to help you describe the part of the island that:
   a) is wettest;
   b) is forested;
   c) has saw mills;
   d) has the best farmland;
   e) is least productive.

2. Draw an outline map of Helicopter Island. Use these symbols on your map to show the best location for a:
   a) lumber town (mark with an **L**);
   b) fishing port (**F**);
   c) gold-mining town (**G**);
   d) ski resort (**S**);
   e) market town (**M**), where farmers bring in their products.

Canada Crossword

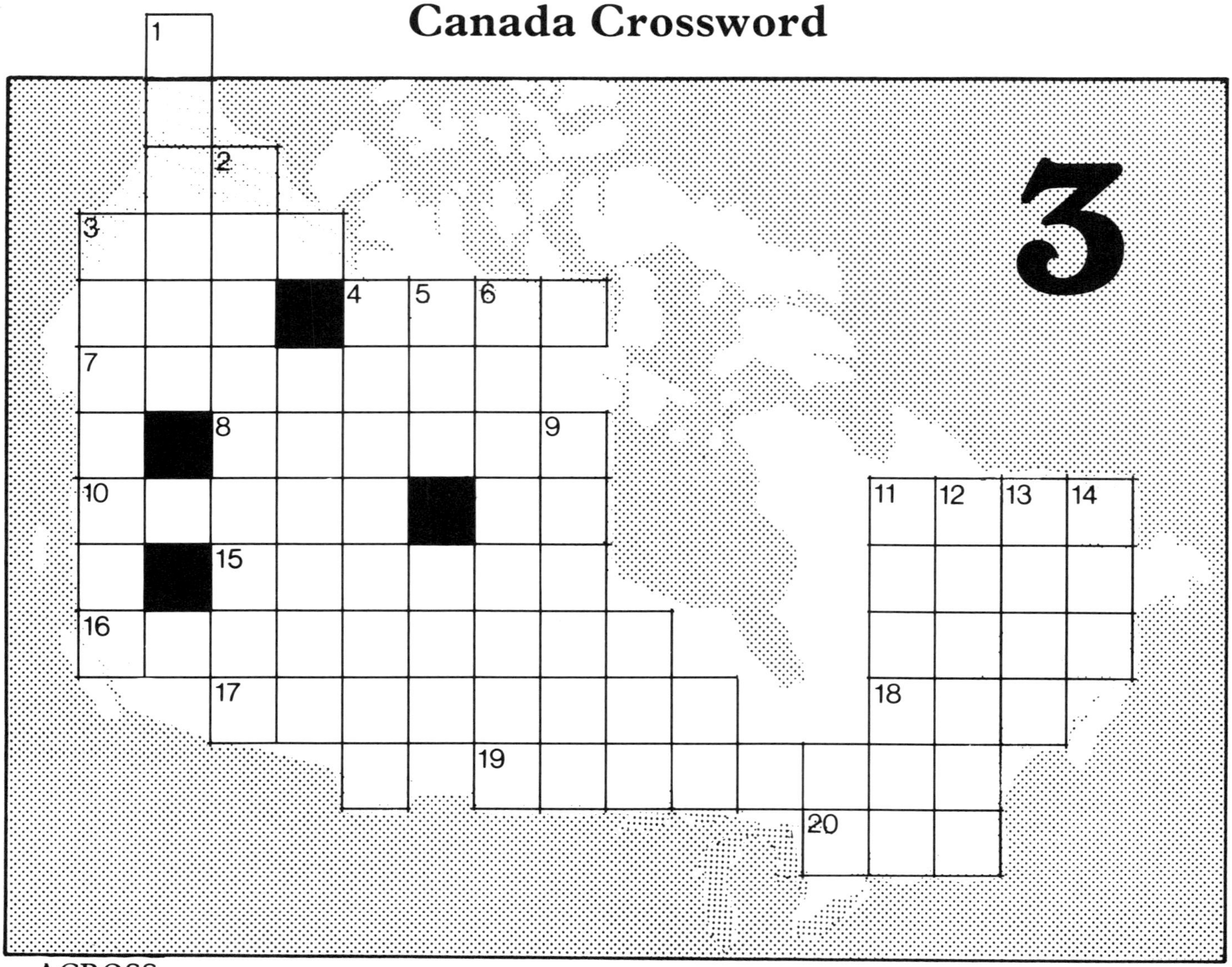

ACROSS

3 Pointed top of a mountain or hill

4 Raised part of the land, smaller than a mountain

7 Canada is in the continent of North ______________

8 Key that explains the symbols on a map

10 Way or route by land

11 Any mark used to represent or point out something

15 Low land between hills or mountains

16 Height above sea level

17 Large city on the St. Lawrence River

18 Inlet of a sea or lake, smaller than a gulf

19 Province between Manitoba and Quebec

20 Not young, worn by age or use

DOWN

1 Small body of flowing water

2 Body of water surrounded by land

3 Level or rolling land with grass, but few or no trees

4 High, hilly region

5 Frozen water

6 Solid part of the earth's surface

9 Time of light between sunrise and sunset

11 Something that stands for, or represents something else

12 Body of land smaller than a continent, completely surrounded by water

13 Shade between black and white

14 Recently grown or made, not old

Using Scale

This cut-away or side view of Canada is called a cross-section or profile.

Colour or shade the part that shows land. The height or elevation is not drawn to scale; only the east-west distance.

How much closer is Winnipeg to the Pacific Ocean than it is to the Atlantic Ocean?

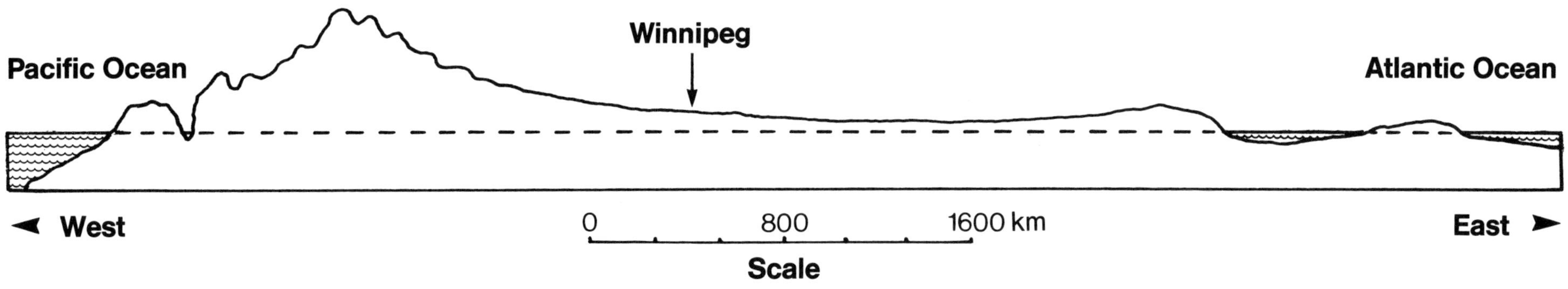

Through 50° North Latitude

Comparing a Map at Different Scales

Maps are scale drawings of part of the earth. It would be almost impossible to draw a map of a place at exactly the same size as the place really is. So, map makers let a small length on the map, such as a centimetre, stand for, or represent, the same distance on the ground, such as a kilometre. The map scale tells how much the map has been reduced in size from the part of the earth it represents. When you change the scale on a map, its shape or area basically remains the same. Only its size changes.

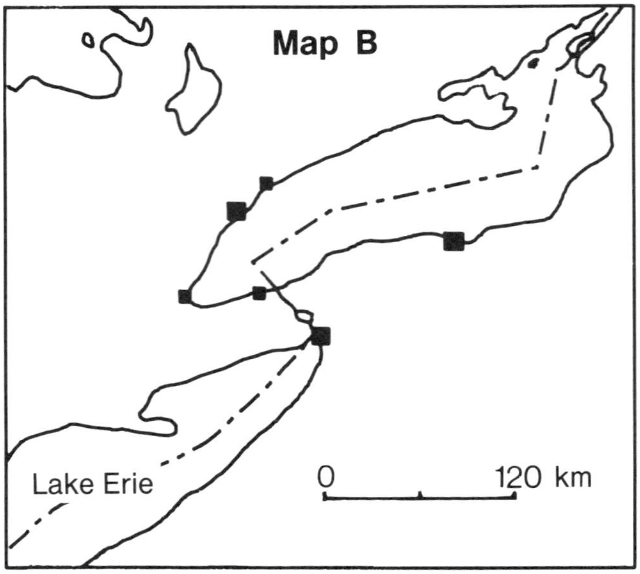

1. Which part of Canada is shown in Map **A**? ______________________
2. Make a legend beside Map **A** to show which is land and which is water.
3. On Map **A**, mark the name of:
   - another lake
   - two countries
   - one province and one state
   - three large cities
4. When you compare Maps **A**, **B**, and **C**, is their area the same, or is their size the same?

   ____

5. Why is the scale different on each map?

   ____

   ______________________.

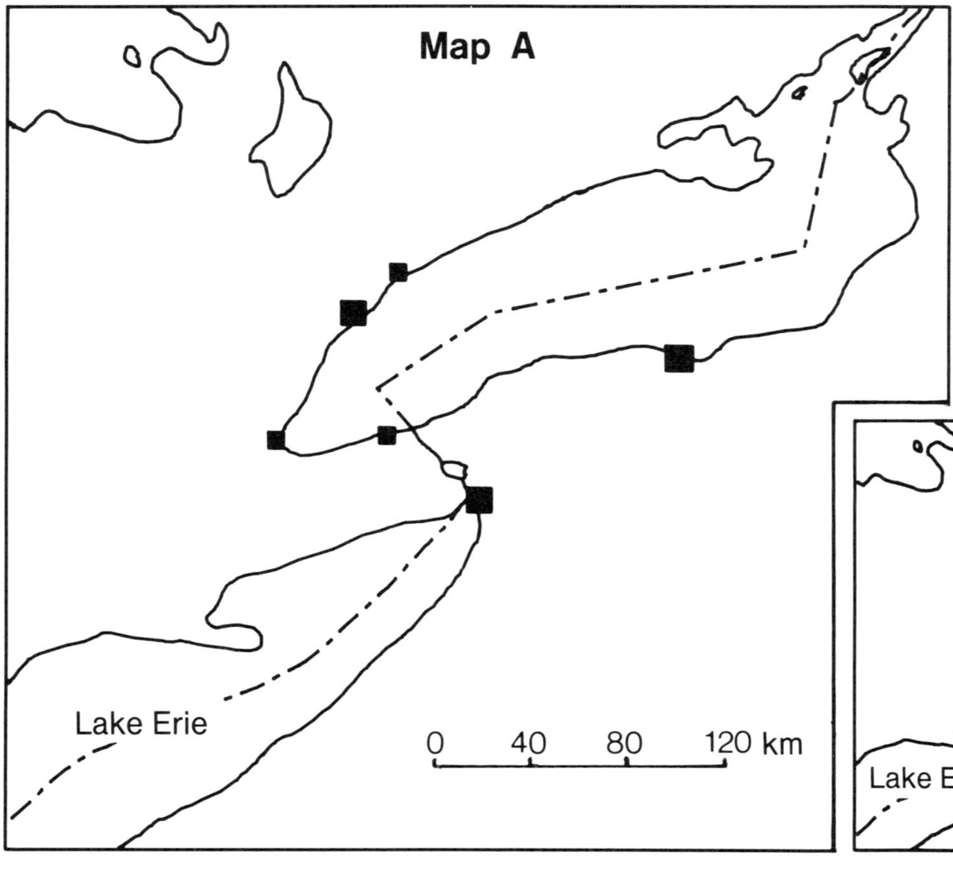

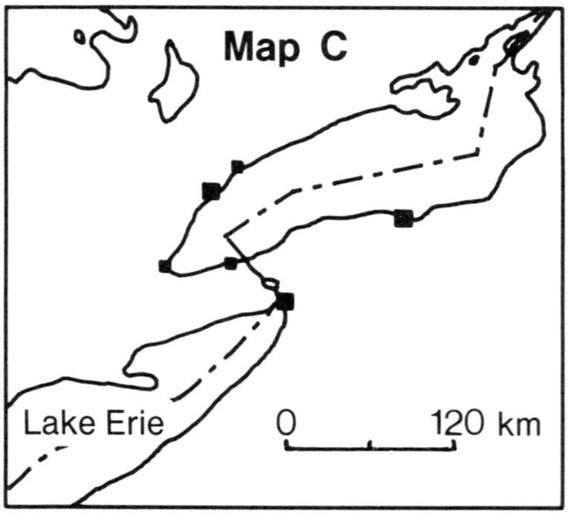

Measuring Straight-Line Distances

Every map should have a scale. The scale shows that a certain length on the map represents a certain distance on the earth. The scale tells how much the map has been reduced in size from the area it represents.

One kind of scale is called a bar scale. A bar scale is like a ruler or measuring tape. The bar scale on Map **D** is shown like this:

0 200 400 km

This means that each 2 cm on the map represents 200 km on that part of the earth called Ontario.

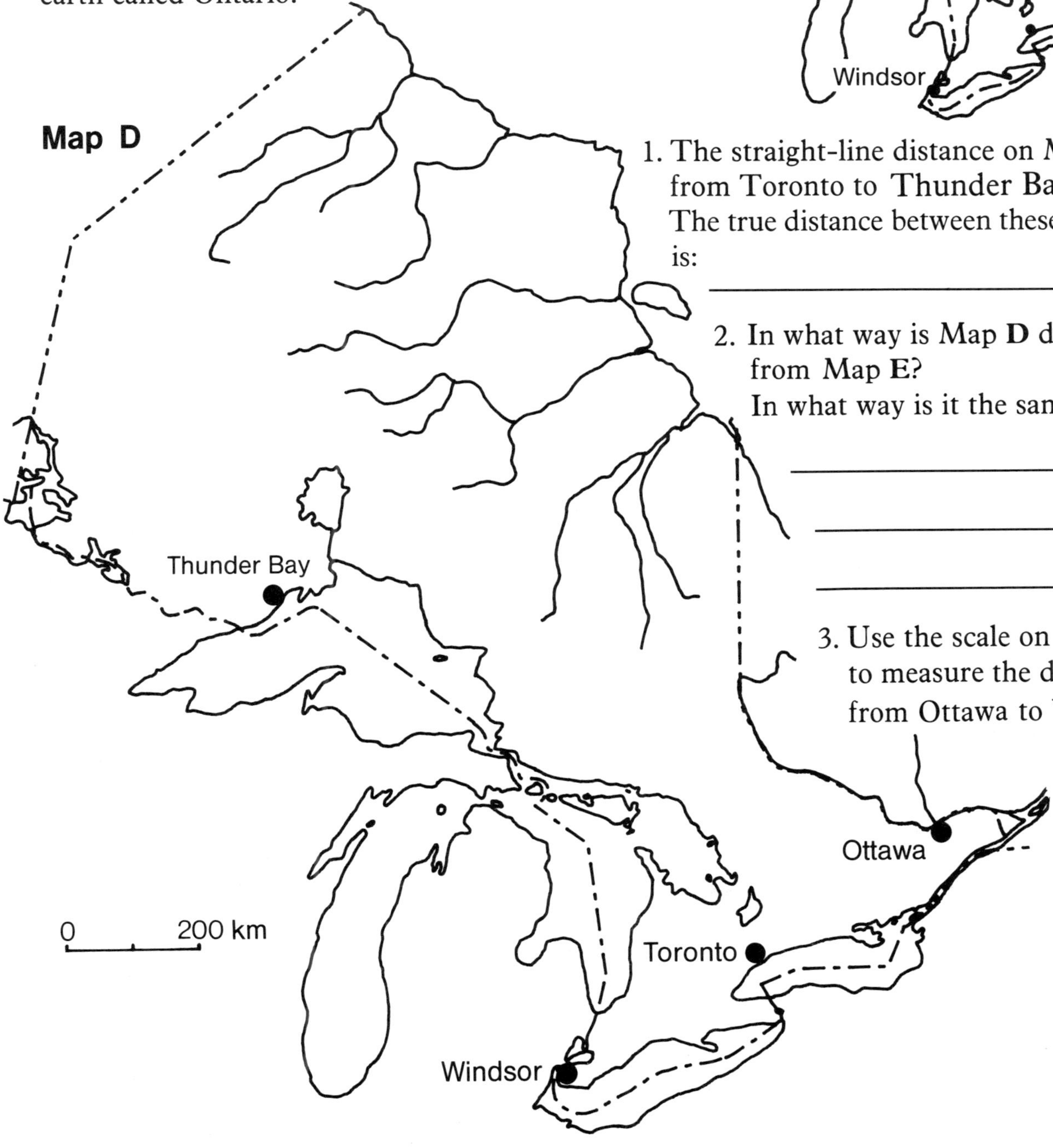

1. The straight-line distance on Map **D** from Toronto to Thunder Bay is 9 cm. The true distance between these two cities is: ____________________

2. In what way is Map **D** different from Map **E**?
   In what way is it the same?
   ____
   ____
   ____

3. Use the scale on each map to measure the distance from Ottawa to Windsor.

Reading Different Map Scales

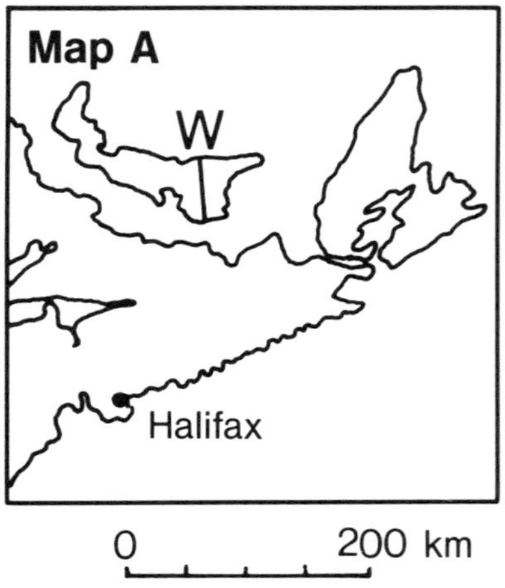

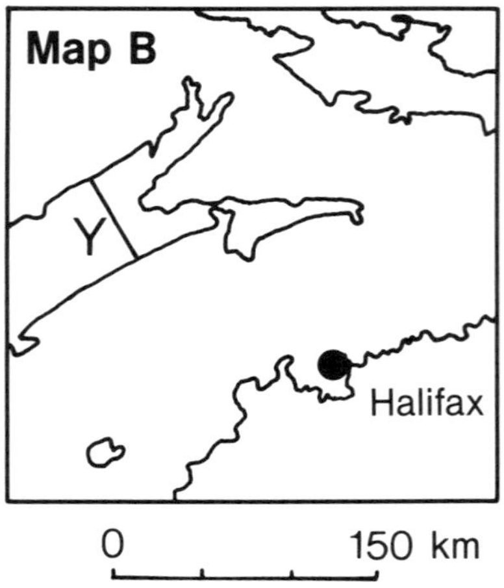

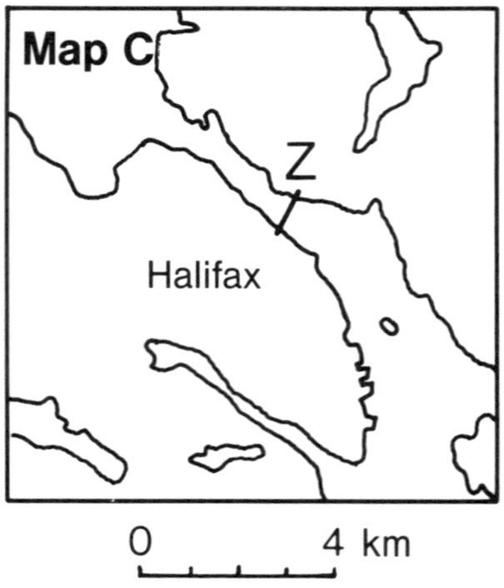

Each map shows the city of Halifax at a different scale.

1. Which map shows Halifax from the highest height or altitude?

____

2. Which map shows the city at the lowest height and in the greatest detail?

____

3. Name correctly on Map **D**:
   - two provinces
   - one gulf
   - one ocean.
   - one strait
   - another city

4. Measure these distances using the correct map scale:
   a) the width of the island at W in Map **A**; _______________
   b) the width across the bay at Y in Map **B**; _______________
   c) the length of the bridge at Z in Map **C**. _______________

5. Map **D** below also shows the position of Halifax.
   Circle the scale that is correct.

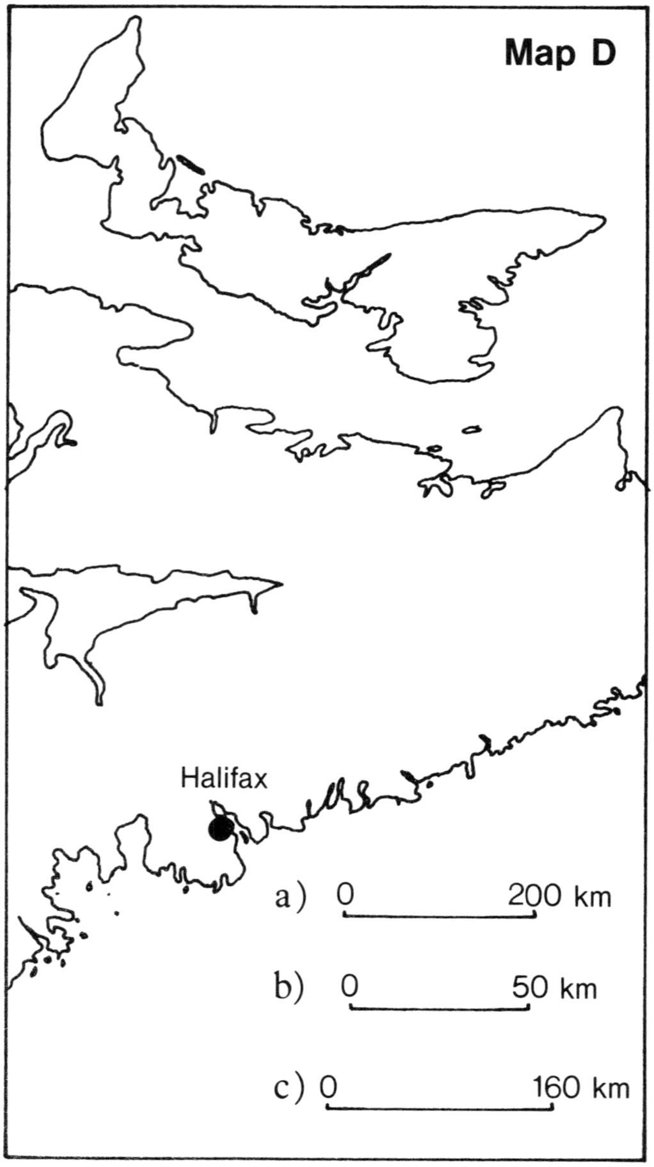

Relating Scale to Area

1	2
This map shows the **largest** area.	This map shows the **smallest** area.

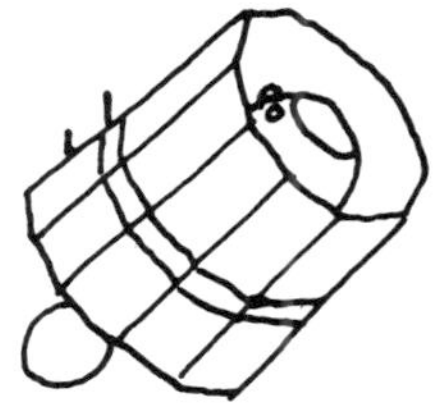

Cut out the **two** maps below that best fit into the above squares.
Put each map in its proper square.

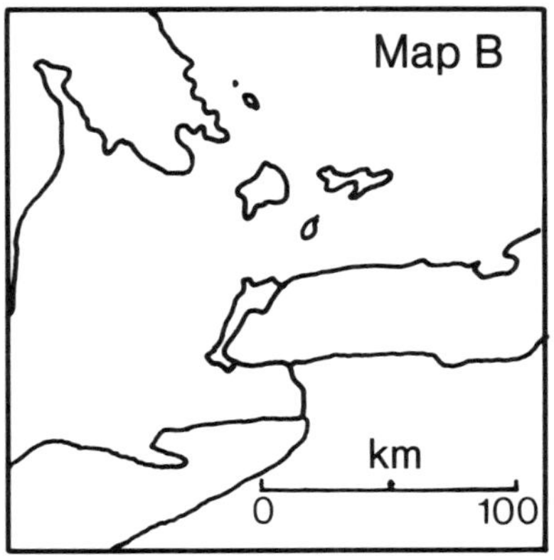

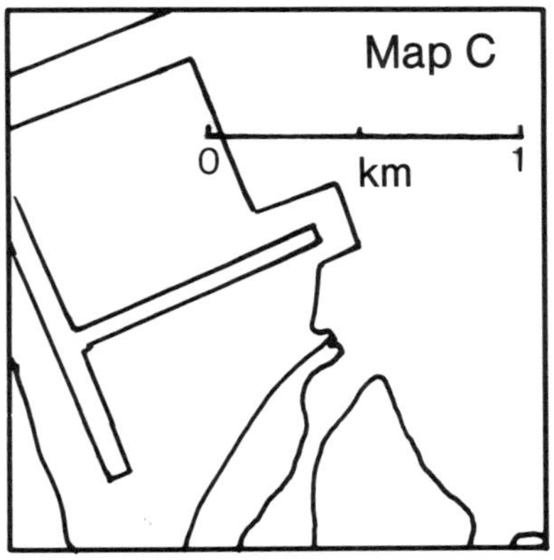

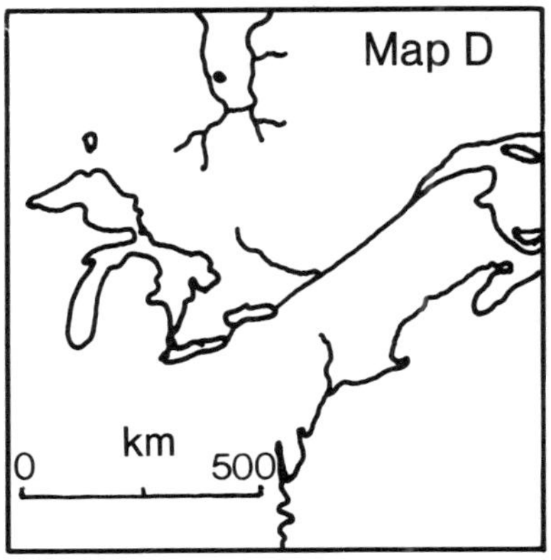

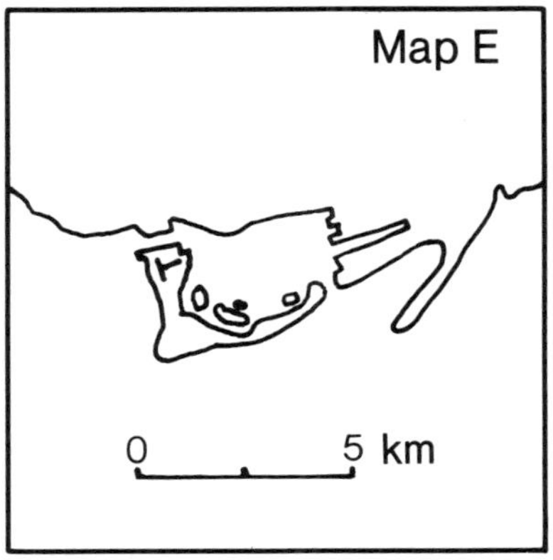

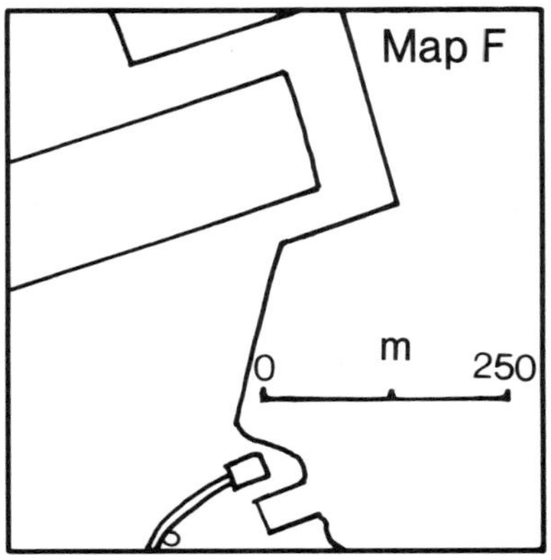

Using Scale to Find Area

The scale compares the size of the drawings of the house with its real size. The scale states that one centimetre on the drawing stands for, or represents, one metre on the ground.

Scale on a map or drawing can be shown in three different ways.

a) 0 1 2 m

b) $\frac{1\text{ cm}}{1\text{ m}}$ $\frac{1}{100}$

c) 1 cm: 1 m 1:100

This symbol, **:** is the short form for "represents".

3. Is the height of the front door 2, 3, or 4 metres?

____

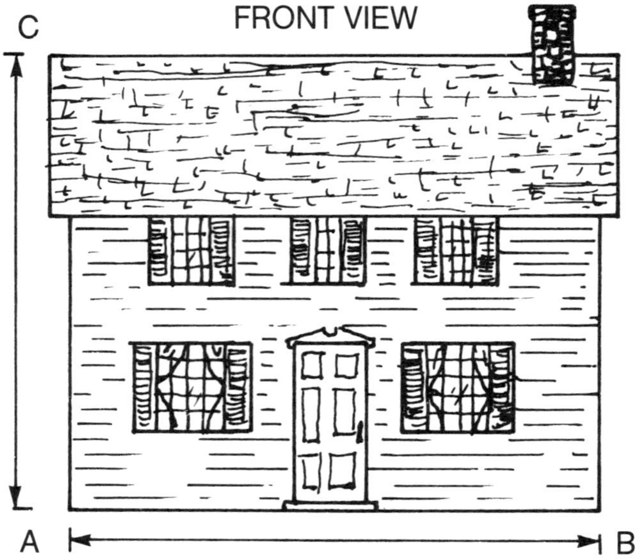

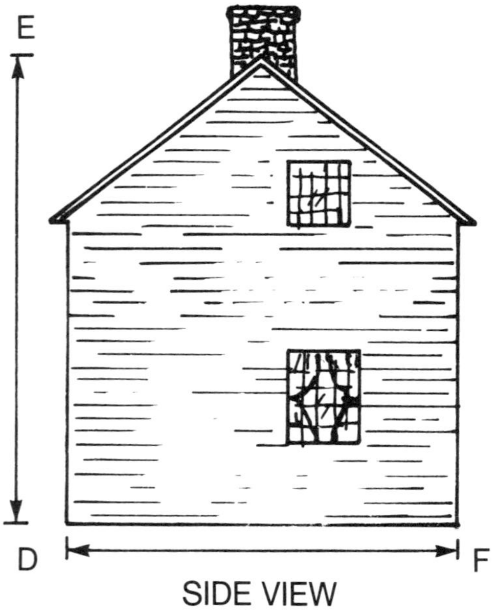

1. Use the front view to measure the distance from A to B.
   Use the scale to find the actual length of the house.

____

2. Measure the height of the house from A to C. Use the scale to find the **actual** height. ______________________

4. Use the scale to find the height of the house from D to E.

____

Use the scale to find the width from D to F.

____

Using Scale to Find Area

5. Use the scale to find the size or area (length x width) of each of the three rooms on the lower floor plan. Put your answers in the proper circles.

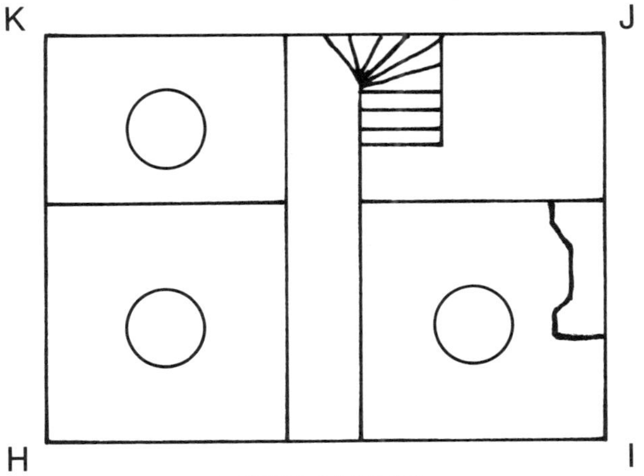

LOWER LEVEL

6. Find the total area of the lower level – H I J K.

Total area of lower level: ◯ square metres.

7. Use the scale to find the area of each room on the upper floor plan. Put your answers in the circles.

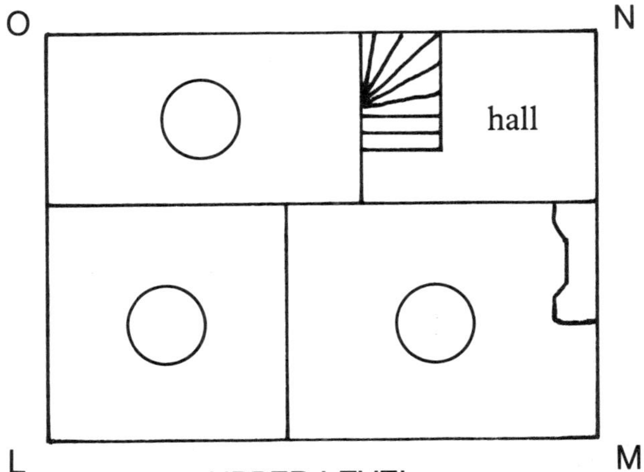

UPPER LEVEL

8. Find the total area of the upper level – L M N O. Put your answer in the circle.

Total area of upper level: ◯ square metres.

9. Use your answers in questions 7 and 8 to find the area of the upper hall and the stairs.

Total area of upper hall and stairs: ◯ square metres.

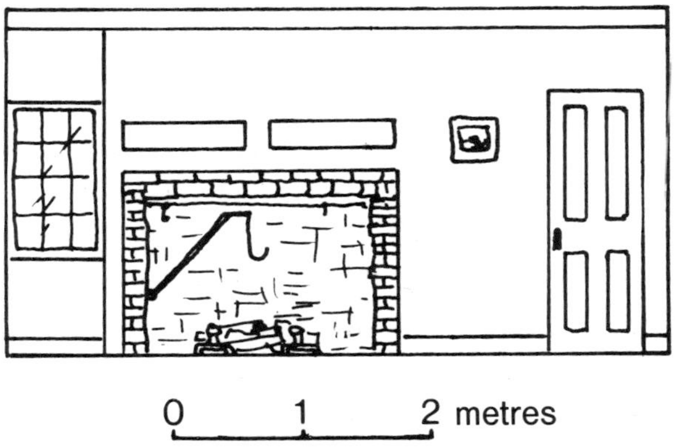

Scale

10. In one of the rooms is a large fireplace. Underline the correct sentence. Use the map scale to help you you decide.

a) The fireplace is 1½ m wide and 1 m high.
b) The fireplace is 3 m wide and 2 m high.
c) The fireplace is 2 m wide and about 1½ m high.

Choosing the Correct Scale

Fort Prince of Wales was a Hudson's Bay Company post located on Hudson Bay at the mouth of the Churchill River. Its founder was a trader named Richard Norton. He established the post to deal with the trade of the company as far as the Lake Athabaska region. This fort was in operation from 1731 until 1782. At this time the English and the French wanted control of the trade in the rich fur country surrounding Hudson Bay. Fort Prince of Wales was built to withstand any French attack.

When it was completed in 1771, it was a huge stone fort, approximately 95 metres square, with bastions at each corner. Its walls (at **H** and **K**) were nearly ten metres thick. There were forty guns at various points in the walls. Surprisingly enough, the fortress surrendered to the French in 1782 without a fight. The Hudson's Bay Company had not placed enough men in the fort to man the guns! All those present in the fort were taken prisoner by the French and carried away in the French ships. As hard as they tried the French were not able to destroy this fortress. They had to content themselves with destroying the guns and blowing holes in the walls that surrounded the fort.

The following year the British returned to Hudson Bay, but they never reoccupied this fort. Perhaps they were too embarrassed!

Which map plan shows Fort Prince of Wales at the correct scale?
Check the above information for an important clue.

____

FORT PRINCE OF WALES

Map A

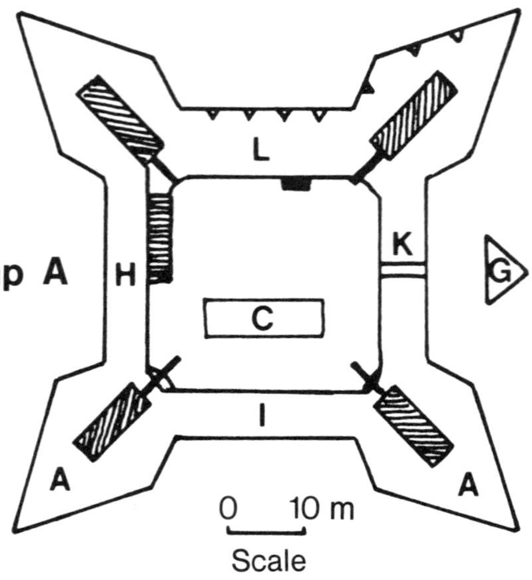

Map B

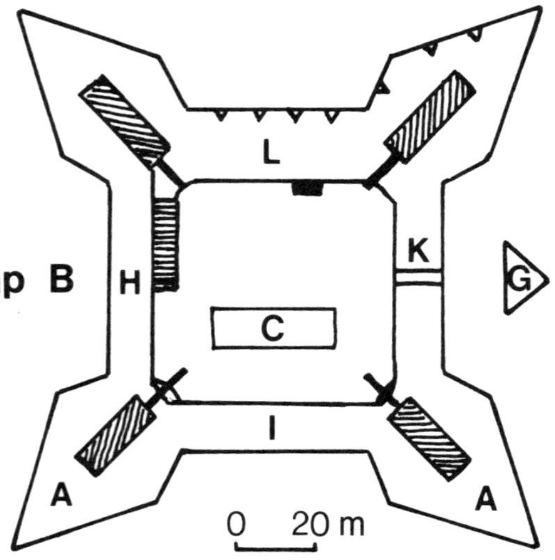

Map C

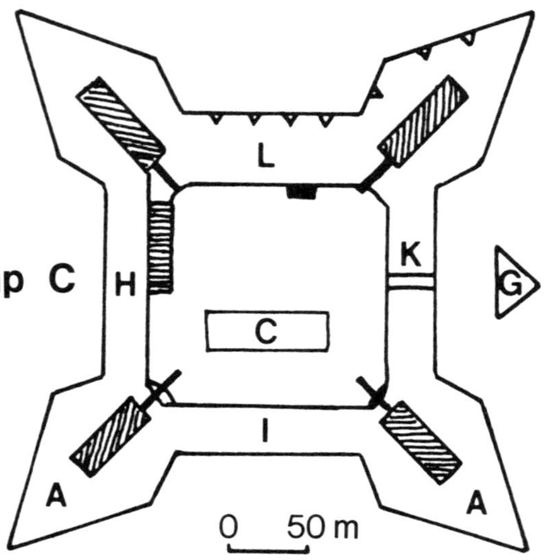

Finding the Shortest Route

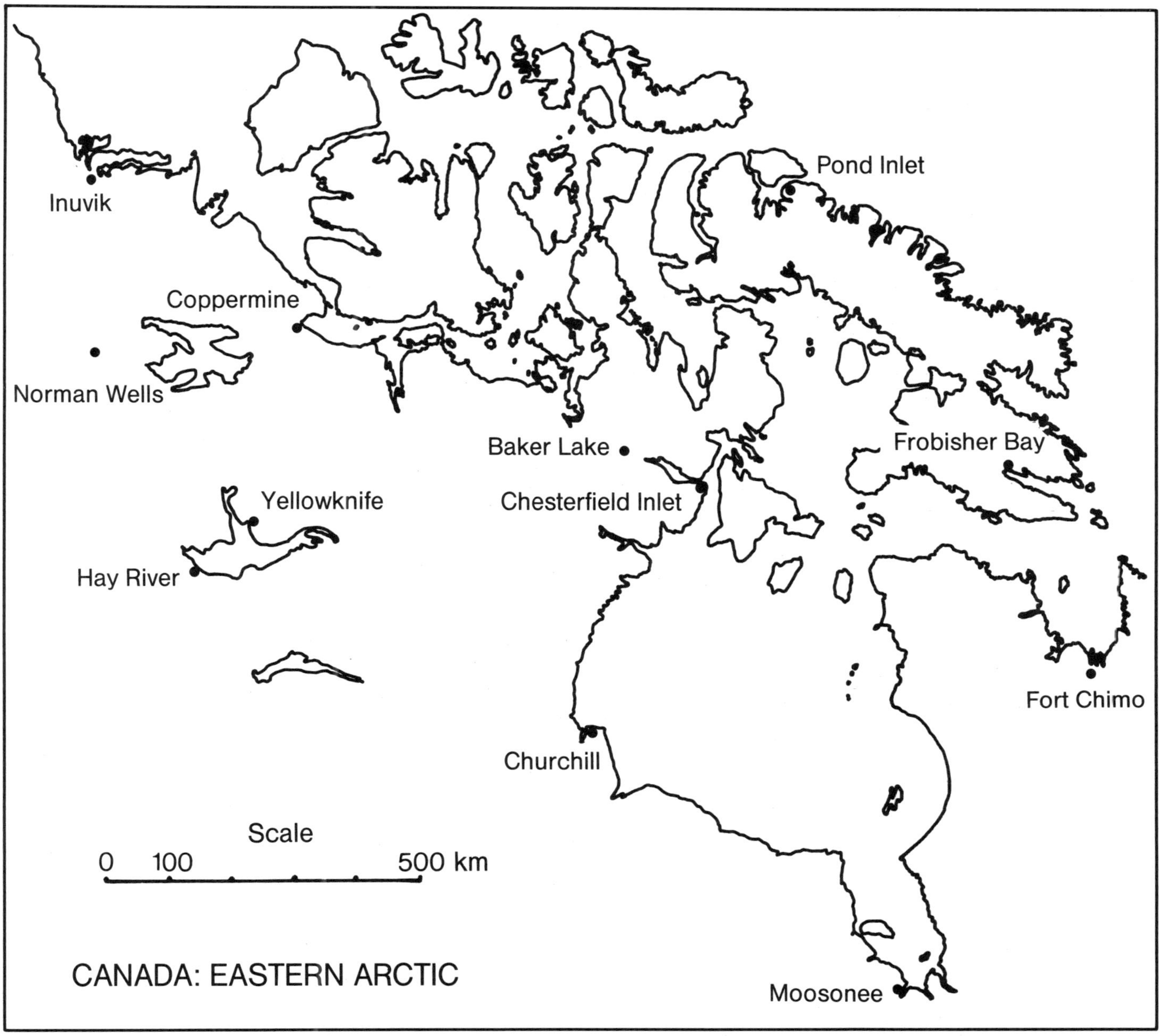

Can you show on the map a way to visit all twelve places without travelling more than 10 200 kilometres?
You must begin and end your journey at the same place.

Measuring Irregular Distances

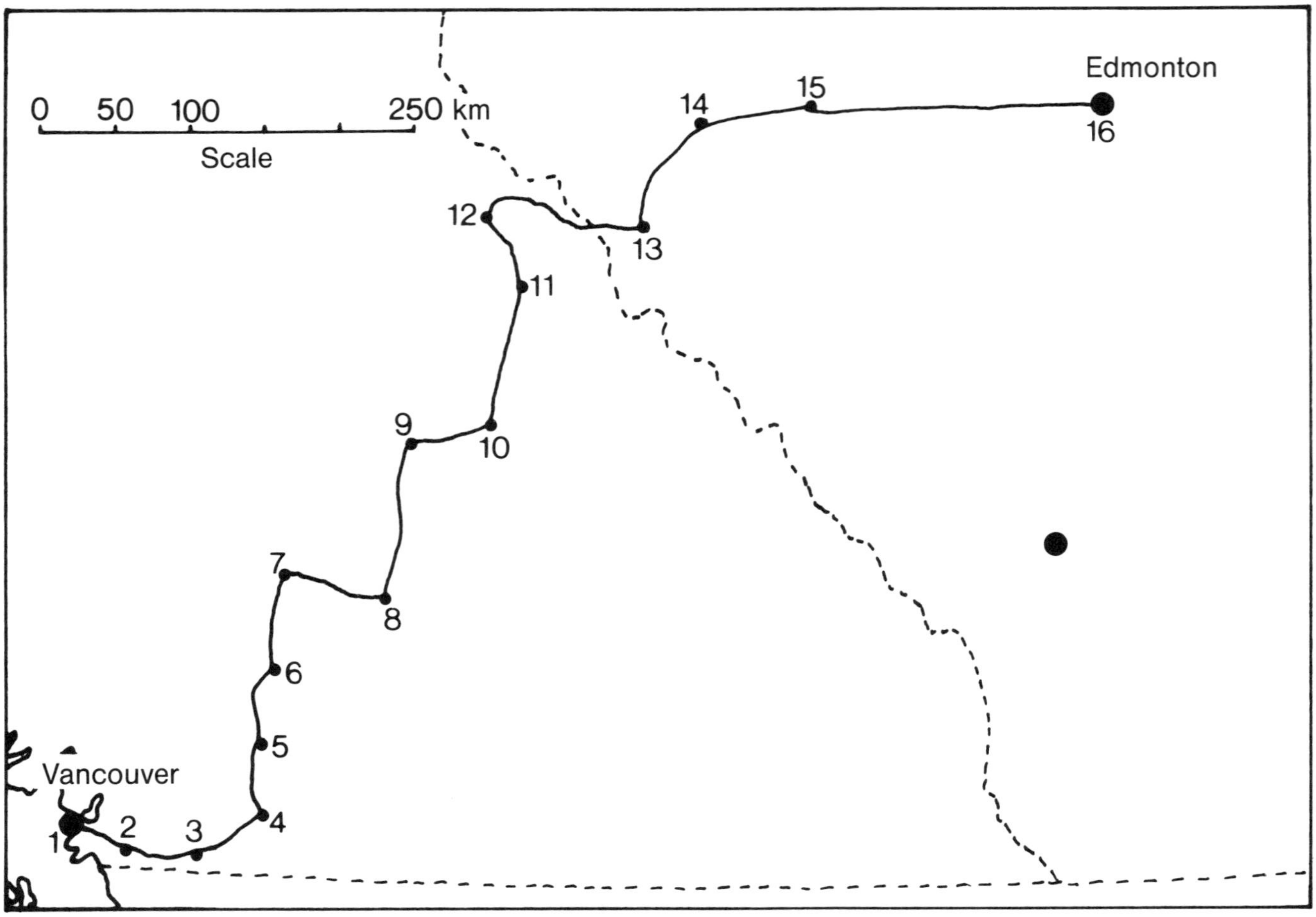

How much longer is the distance by road than it is by air between Vancouver and Edmonton?

Road distance: ____________________

Air or straight-line distance: ____________________

Difference: ____________________

Clue: Use this method to measure broken or irregular distances on a map:

a) Place the edge of a piece of paper on the map along line 1-2.

b) Mark point 1 and point 2 on the paper. This gives you the distance between the two points.

c) Turn the edge of the paper along line 2-3.

d) Start at 2 and make another mark on the paper at 3. This gives you the distance along the edge of the paper between points 2 and 3.

e) Continue to measure and record each distance until you finish line 15-16.

f) Now measure the entire distance on your paper between points 1 and 16.

Map Mystery

Many years ago there lived two stage coach drivers. Each boasted of the great distance that he travelled every day. One day, in the middle of their talk, an elderly gentleman interrupted. "Sirs", he said, "whoever drives the longer distance will get this gold coin. But you must prove how far you travel. You must show me a map of your route."

That evening, each driver made a map of his route and gave it to the gentleman. Carefully, he studied the two maps. Then, he handed a gold coin to the first driver.

Had the gentleman made a mistake? Measure the distance along each route to check.

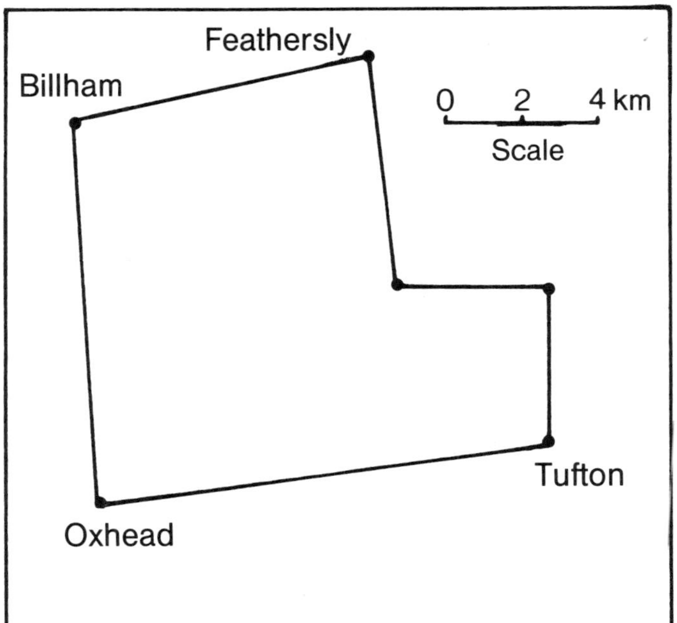

FIRST DRIVER'S MAP

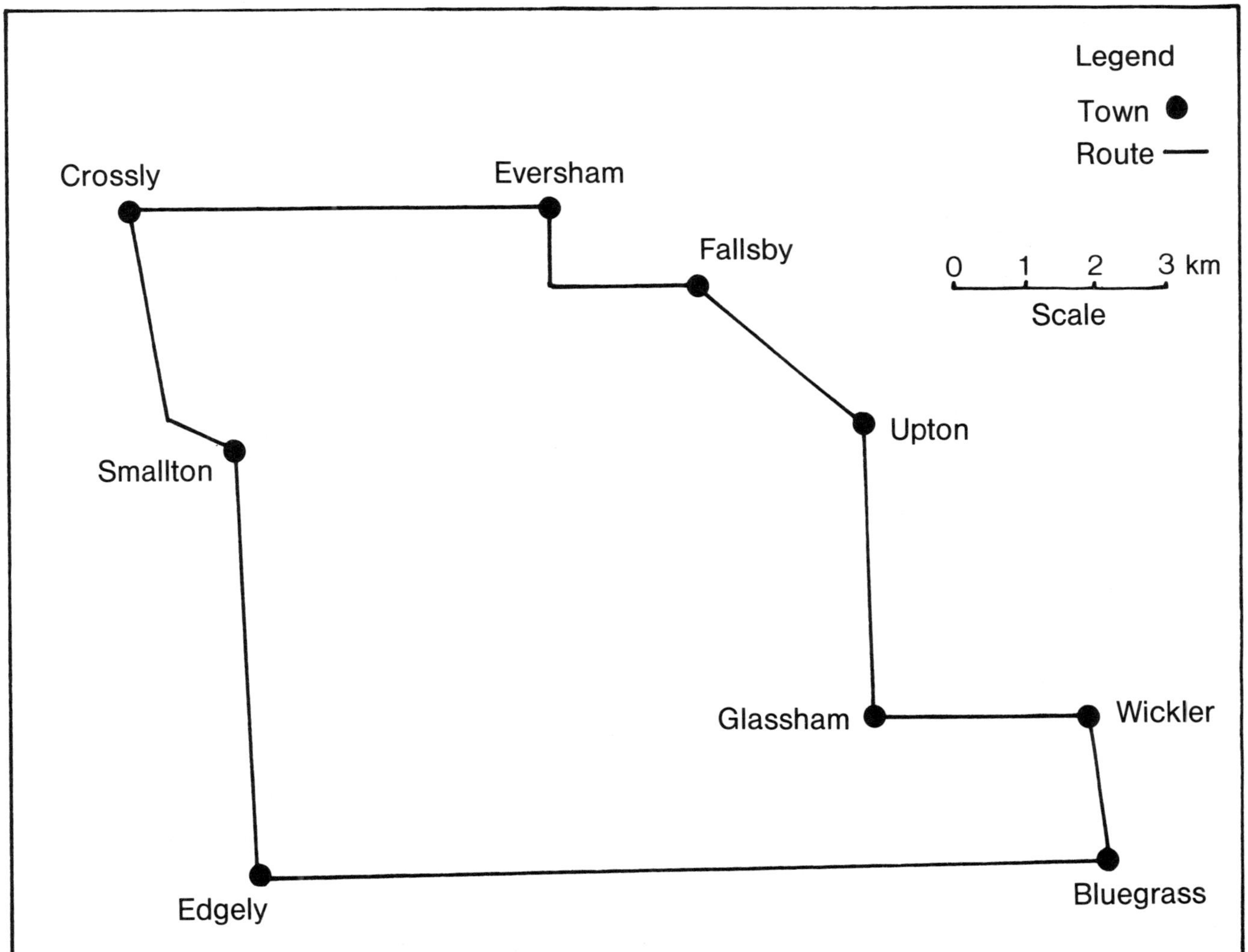

SECOND DRIVER'S MAP

Choosing the Best Location

You are to decide the best location for a new airport. The place you choose must:
- be no more than 15 minutes by car from the edge of the cities;
- be no closer than 6 km from a hospital or zoo;
- have a runway at least 4 km long;
- have the runway on flat land;
- allow pilots to approach the runway from east or west.

Examine the symbols on the map and in the legend to help you decide. Then put an X on the map to show the best location for the airport.

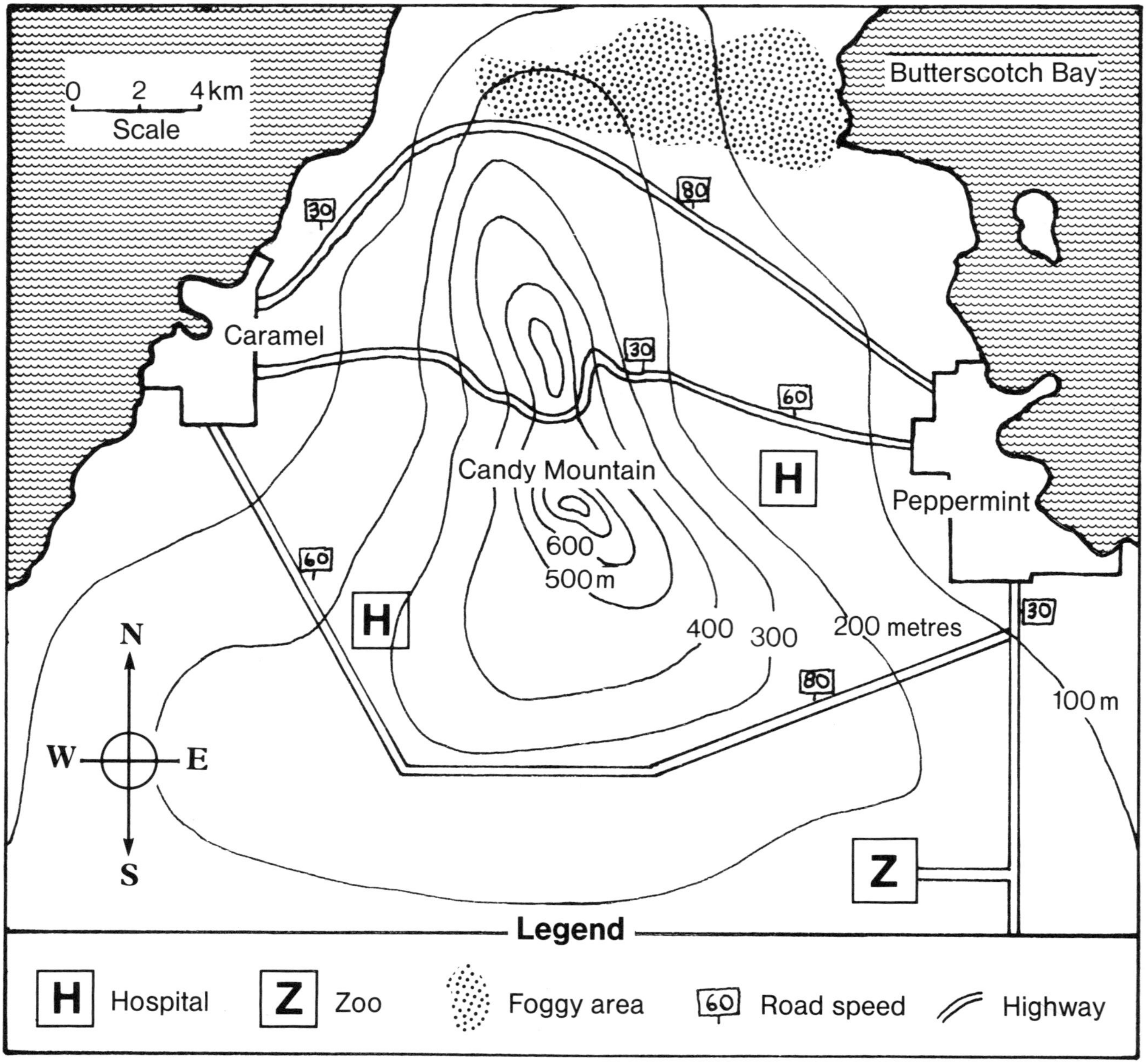

Choosing the Best Route

The fur trade was probably fatal for the colony of New France. In a way, it drained the colony of its men and its resources. Farming was never as profitable as the fur trade. Many young men left the little settlements along the St. Lawrence to make their fortunes as fur traders in the interior of Canada. These traders became known as 'coureurs-de-bois' or 'runners of the woods'. They frequently lived with the native people of the region and adopted their customs. The loss of these young men weakened the struggling colony of New France.

Also, the far-ranging explorations of the French traders led the French to claim more land than they could defend. The English settlement of the Thirteen Colonies proved that only populated land was secure against attack. The French could not hope to save the Mississippi Valley for the fur trade in the face of English settlers who wanted the land.

The fur trade helped shape New France, but in the end it hurt the colony. It made enemies of the powerful Iroquois. It led the French to claim more land in North America than they could ever hope to settle and to defend. And finally, it attracted men into the wilderness who might have become farmers and family men. That the French were eventually defeated was in part due to their involvement in the fur trade.

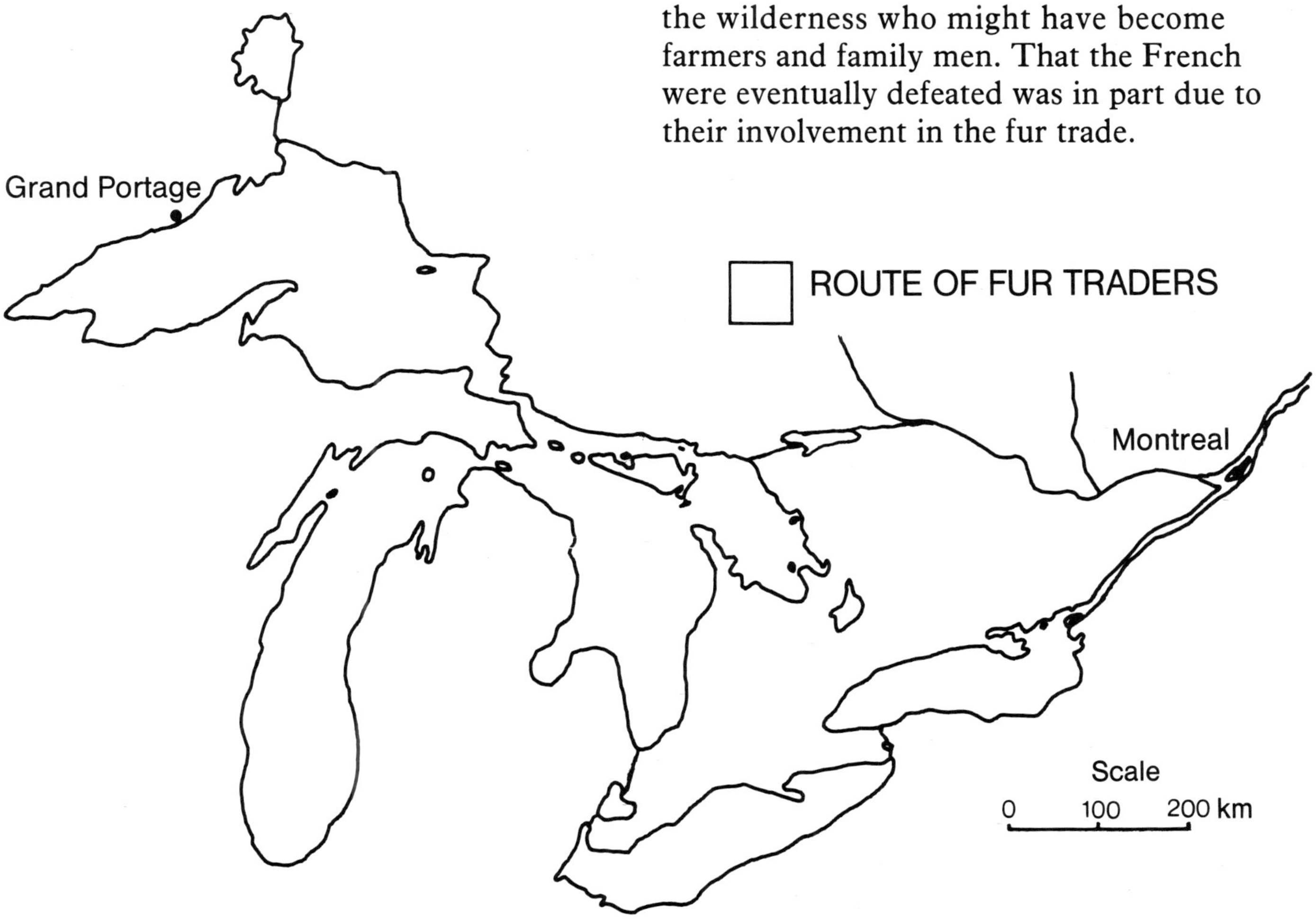

Show on the map the "best" route for the fur traders to follow between Montreal and Grand Portage. Remember, they travelled by canoe and were seldom out of sight of land. Use the scale to calculate the distance by water between Montreal and Grand Portage.

Canada Crossword

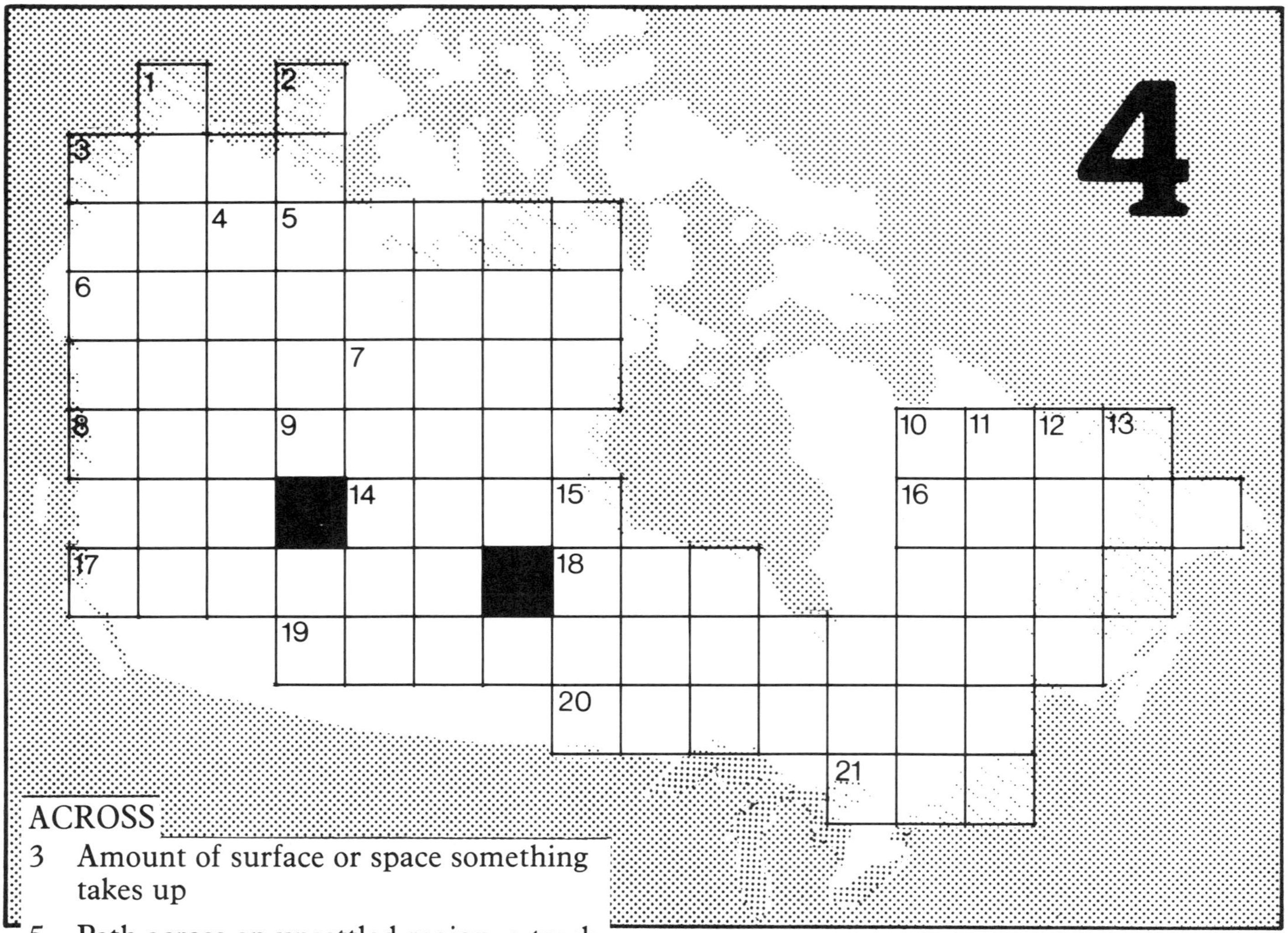

ACROSS

3 Amount of surface or space something takes up

5 Path across an unsettled region, a track

6 Ocean between Europe and Africa, and the Americas

7 Broad, not narrow

8 Last part, edge, or boundary

9 A long, narrow mark

10 Water falling in drops from the clouds

14 Very small amount of liquid, shaped like a ball

16 Below, beneath

17 How long a thing is

18 Abbreviation or short form for Ontario

19 Capital city of the Yukon

20 To find out the size, amount, length, or width of anything

21 Long pole with a flat blade at one end for rowing or steering a boat

DOWN

1 A long way, far away

2 To tell or describe item by item

3 Size of a map compared to what it represents

4 Move smoothly and easily over a surface

7 How wide a thing is, the distance across

10 Straight strip of wood or metal, marked in units, used to draw lines or measure

11 Speak or write words in return to a question

12 Plan, picture, belief in the mind, a thought

13 Not existing before

15 Form of writing in verse that expresses imaginative thought or strong feeling

Landforms in Picture and Map

Can you name the **seven** landforms in the picture?

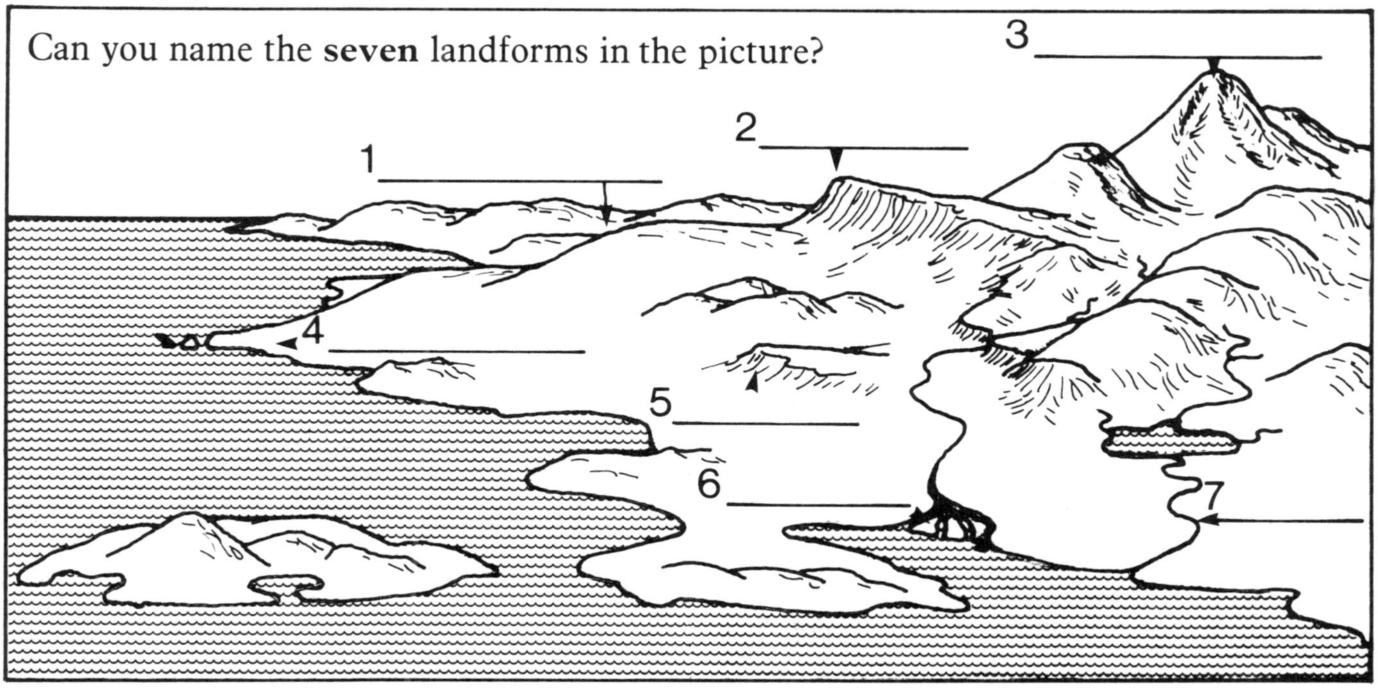

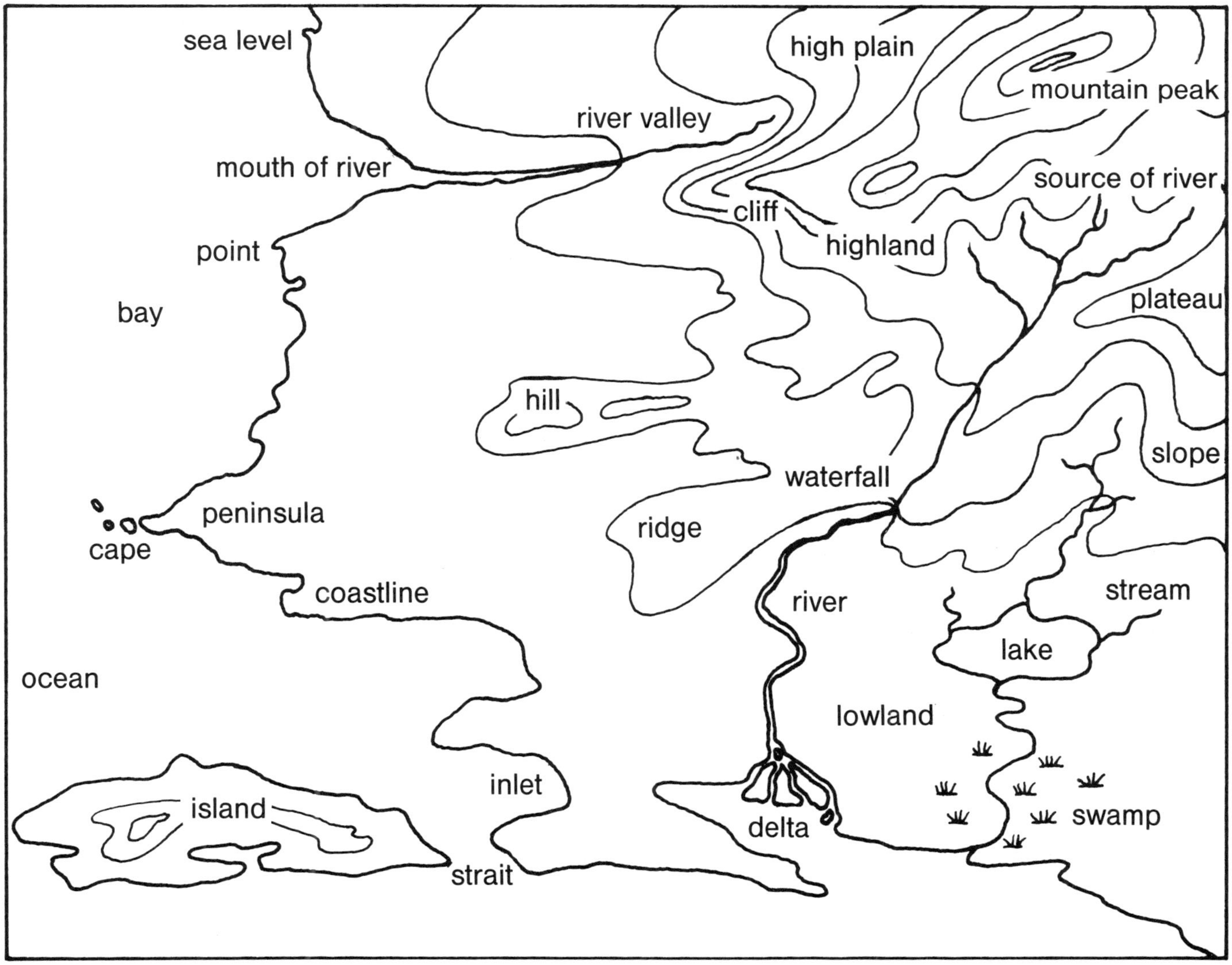

Map and Globe Terms

Area – a region.

Arctic – a region at or near the North Pole; of the north polar region.

Atlas – a book of maps covering a large area or the whole world.

Axis – an imaginary line that runs through the centre of the earth. The North and South Pole are located at either end of the earth's axis.

Bay – part of a sea or lake extending into the land.

Chart – a plan showing air or sea routes.

Continent – one of the seven large land masses of the earth.

Compass – an instrument for showing directions, consisting of a needle that points to the North Magnetic Pole.

Contours – lines joining points on a map that have the same height above sea level.

Cross-section – a profile or side-view of the land showing its height above sea level.

Degree – a unit for measuring the earth's surface. The earth is 360 degrees around.

Delta – An area of land at the mouth of a river, formed by deposits of earth such as sand, and usually in the shape of a triangle.

Dimension – a measurement of length, width, or thickness.

Direction – the way one may face or point; north, south, east, or west.

Distortion – change in the shape of an image or object from its original shape.

Equator – an imaginary circle around the middle of the earth, midway between the North and South Poles. The equator is 0° latitude.

Erosion – the process of wearing away rock by the work of sun, wind, rain, ice, rivers, and the sea, and depositing it elsewhere.

Glacier – great masses of moving ice.

Globe – a sphere representing the earth; a model of the earth.

Grid – two sets of parallel lines evenly spaced and crossing each other. A grid makes it possible to find the exact location of a place.

Gulf – a large bay; an arm of an ocean or sea extending into the land.

Hemisphere – one half of the earth, for example, the part below the equator.

Hill – a high part of the earth's surface, but smaller than a mountain.

Island – land completely surrounded by water but smaller than a continent.

Inset map – a smaller map inserted or placed within the border of a larger map.

Key (map) – a part of the map which explains the abbreviation or symbols (colours, lines, and figures) used on the map.

Landform – any feature of the landscape that is caused by nature.

Latitude – Lines of latitude or parallels are imaginary circles running east-west around the earth. Distance north or south on the earth's surface is measured in degrees of latitude.

Legend – or key; words accompanying a picture, map, or diagram.

Longitude – Lines of longitude, or meridians, are imaginary lines running from the North Pole to the South Pole. Distance east or west on the earth's surface is measured in degrees of longitude.

Map – a flat drawing representing certain features of the earth's surface or part of it.

Mountain – a mass of land that rises very high above the land around it.

Map and Globe Terms

Mouth (river) – the part of a river where its waters empty into another body of water.

North Pole – the point farthest north on the earth's surface.

Ocean – one of the four great bodies of salt water that covers nearly three-fourths of the earth's surface.

Peninsula – a point of land that sticks out from a larger body of land and is almost entirely surrounded by water.

Plain – a flat stretch of land, prairie.

Plateau – a large, high plain in the mountains, or at a height above sea level.

Pole – the point at either end of the earth's axis.

Port – a place where boats can anchor and be safe from storms; a harbour.

Prime Meridian – an imaginary line from the North Pole to the South Pole through Greenwich, England. Longitude is measured east or west of this line. The Prime meridian, or first meridian, is 0° longitude.

Position – the place where something is located.

Profile – an outline of land as seen from the side; a cross-section or side view.

Proportion – the relation of one thing compared to another in size, number, amount, or degree.

Relief – describes the shape of the land and landforms.

Route – a way to go or travel between two points.

Scale – the size of a map, plan, drawing, or model compared to what it represents.

Segment – a section of a sphere or circle.

Slope – a stretch of rising or falling land.

South Pole – the point farthest south on the earth's surface.

Sphere – any rounded shape like a ball.

Symbol – a drawing or figure which stands for, or represents a feature or idea.

Weathering – the gradual breakdown of rocks by wind, water, and temperature changes.

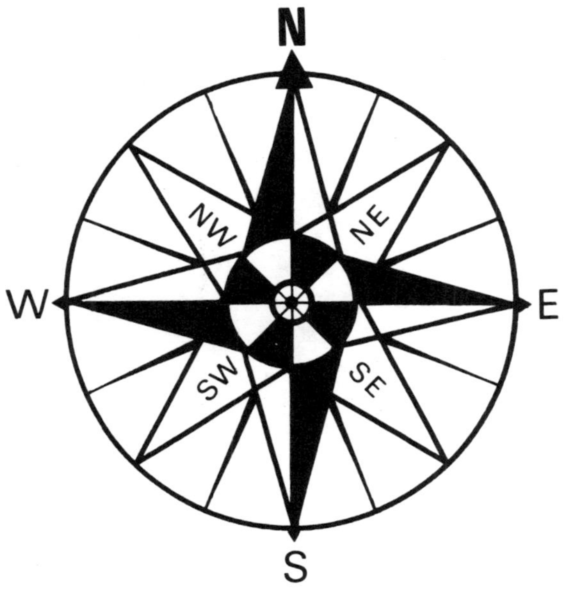

Answers and Solutions

5. Map A

6. Picture C

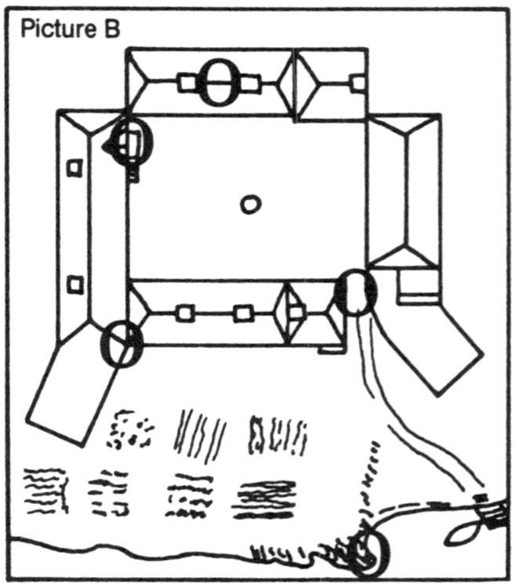

7. 2. A map shows things at same size and in same position as overhead view. 3. A map shows only important (stationary) features and does not show depth.

8. 1. A 4. a) map b) map; less bulky c) map view

10. 3. . . . divides the globe into two equal parts or hemispheres—northern and southern. 4. South America, Africa 5. North America

11. 1. Their shape and size are different 2. Map B 3. Only a globe shows the earth's curved surface without distorting shape and area. 4. navigation charts, route maps 5. density and distribution maps; land use, vegetation, rainfall . . .

12. On this map, Great Slave Lake becomes a flying goose, Lake Winnipeg turns into a standing fox, and Hudson Bay takes the shape of a plump rabbit whose tail is James Bay and whose ears are the southern part of Baffin Island.

13. 1-A 2-B 3-D 4-E 5-F

14. Shapes B, D, and I are incorrect.

15. 1—James Bay
2—Gulf of St. Lawrence
3—Lake Superior
4—Lake Erie
5—Great Bear Lake
6—Ungava Bay
7—Lake Ontario
8—Lake Nipigon (N. Ont.)
9—Bay of Fundy
10—Lake Athabaska
11—Lake Winnipeg
12—Lake Huron-Georgian Bay
13—Great Slave Lake
14—Lake Winnipegosis
15—Lake Michigan

17. delta

18.

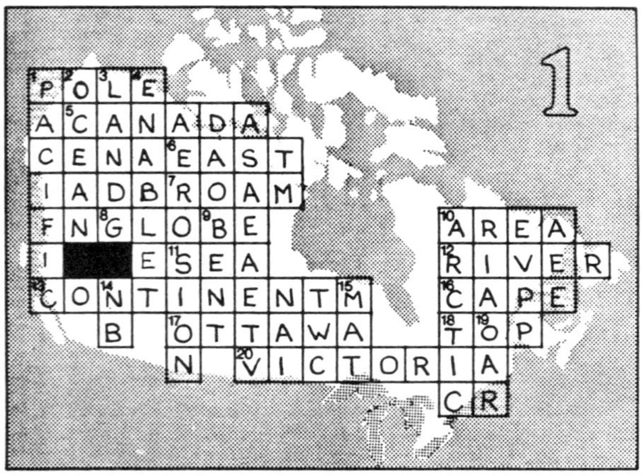

19. Map B. Turn the compass rose around so that the directions are correct.

20. 1. left 2. left

21. 1. farmhouse 2. upper right 3. small barn 4. in front of barn or in upper right part of map 5. Reference points are provided—left, right, upper, lower.

22. 1. Charlottetown 2. a) Summerside b) Murray Harbour c) Borden 3. a) C6 b) D10 c) D7 4. Sherwood 5. C4

23. 1. Osage 2. Weyburn 3. A1 4. May travel through Stoughton or Weyburn. 5. Estevan-L10, Benson-J10, Stoughton-H10, Fillmore-F8, Osage-E7, Lajord-C4, Regina-A1 (May also travel through Weyburn and Corinne.)

24. The compass needle in each airplane points to the north magnetic pole, not to the true north at the North Pole.

25. Hudson Bay

26. 1. B 4. Equator 5. The latitude at the North Pole; at the South Pole.

27. 2. Quito 3. Leningrad 4. Santiago 5. Santiago and Sydney

28. 1. B. 2. B 3. meridians

29. 1. On this map, the longitude lines are straight; they do not come together at the poles as they do on a globe. 4. London 5. Vancouver 6. Adelaide and Tokyo

30. 1) Alert, 2) 45° N, 3) 45° N 76° W, 4) 130° W, 5) St. John's 6) 49° N, 7) Yellowknife, 8) Whitehorse, 9) Windsor, 10) 50° N

31. 1. A—Edmonton, B—Calgary, C—Medicine Hat, D-Regina, E-Saskatoon 2. a) west, b) east, c) west, d) east 3. a) Vancouver, b) Calgary, c) Regina, d) Winnipeg, e) Toronto 4. east, south-east

32.

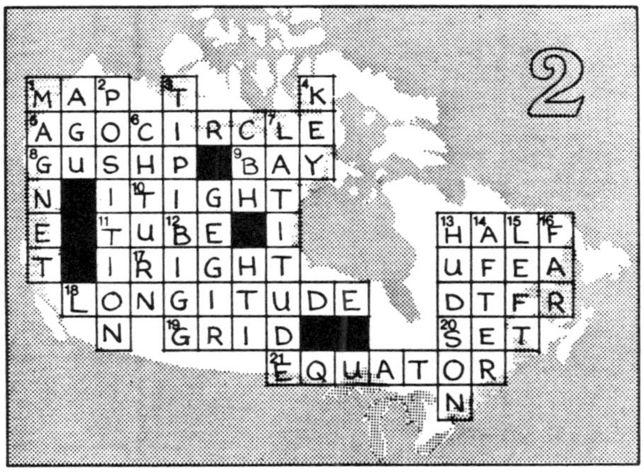

33. whaling and sealing symbol in Prairies, fruit and beef cattle symbols in Arctic, grain in Northern Quebec, vegetables in Atlantic Ocean off Labrador coast

34. 1. a tree or trees 2. a tree, trees

35. cutting down trees, chopping logs for fuel or for building a shelter, hunting animals for food, bringing food (game) back to camp

36. 1. . .the symbols in Map A are explained. 2. Like a key, the legend "unlocks" the information on a map and "opens up" its meaning. 3. land, islands, lakes, bays. 4. The map symbols do not look like the things they represent. 5. The important symbols should be explained in a legend; each symbol should look like the feature it represents.

37. 1. natural symbols—island, hill, forest, beach, waterfall; cultural symbols—town, airport, gold mine, fence, orchard, barn, hospital 2. Edge of Laurentian Shield, Rapids, River

38. 2. Alberta, Saskatchewan, Manitoba 3. 1-Edmonton, 2-Calgary, 3-Saskatoon, 4-Regina, 5-Winnipeg, 6-Peace, 7-Athabaska, 8-North Saskatchewan, 9-Red, 10-Nelson 5. The Prairies: Main Cities and Rivers

39. 1. large dots 2. Saskatchewan 3. cattle-grain, grain-mixed livestock 4. Saskatchewan 5. forest

40. 4. The numbers show the height of land or elevation in metres. 6. A

41. 4. The numbers give the elevation of three mountain peaks. 5. Golden Hinde

42. 1. Atlantic Canada and area 2. The spelling of some place names differs from their present spelling; the coastline is not very accurate; the scale, compass rose, and lettering are shown in an old style. 3. Gulf of St. Lawrence, St. Lawrence River, Sable Island, Bay of Fundy, Quebec, Quebec Province, Nova Scotia

43. Shown is the part of Eastern Canada that was originally explored and settled by Europeans. 1–A 2–C 3–B

44. 1. Lake Athabaska 2. Mackenzie's 1789 route 3. 1793 route 4. Mackenzie R., Arctic 5. west, Rocky Mountains, Coast Mountains

45. 1. a) east, b) east, c) east, d) east, e) west

46.

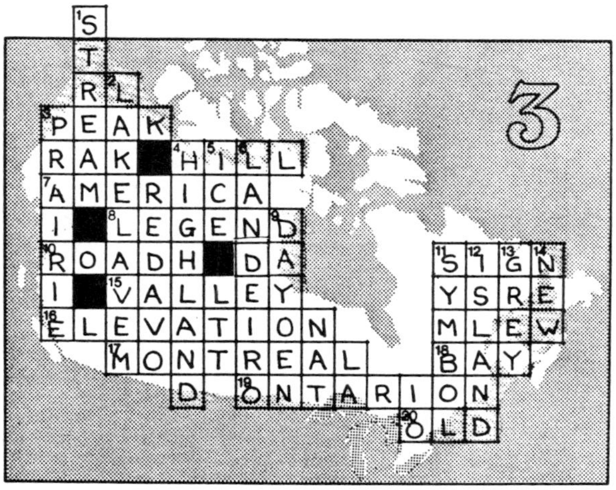

47. 800 km

48. 1. Part of Southern Ontario and New York State 4. Their area is the same. 5. Each map shows the same area but at a different size.

49. 1. 900 km 2. Map D is smaller than Map E. Both maps are at a different scale. Both maps show the same area.
3. 700 kilometres

50. 1. Map A 2. Map C
4. a) 50 km, b) 50 km, c) 1 km
5. b)

51. 1—Map D, 2—Map F

52. 1. A to B is 7 cm, 7 m 2. 6m
3. 2 m 4. 6m, 5m

53. 5. 6 square metres, 9 m^2, 9 m^2 6. 35 m^2
7. 8m^2, 9m^2, 12m^2 8. 35m^2
9. 6m^2 10. c)

54. Map B

55.

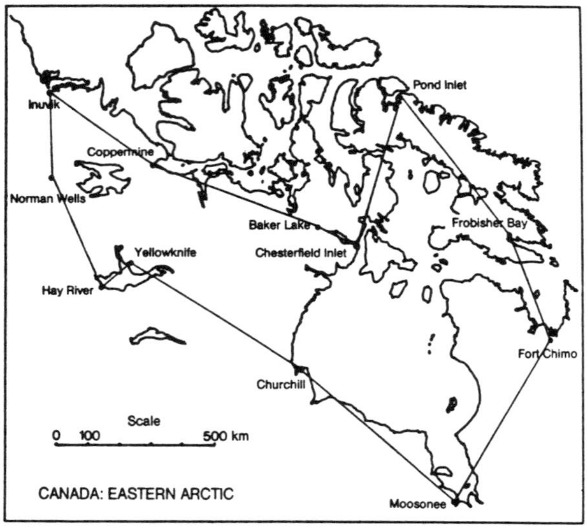

56. Road distance: 23 cm or 1150 km; air distance: 17 cm or 850 km; difference: 300 km

57. No, the gentleman had not made a mistake. The first driver's route covered 44 km; that of the second driver, 43 km.

58.

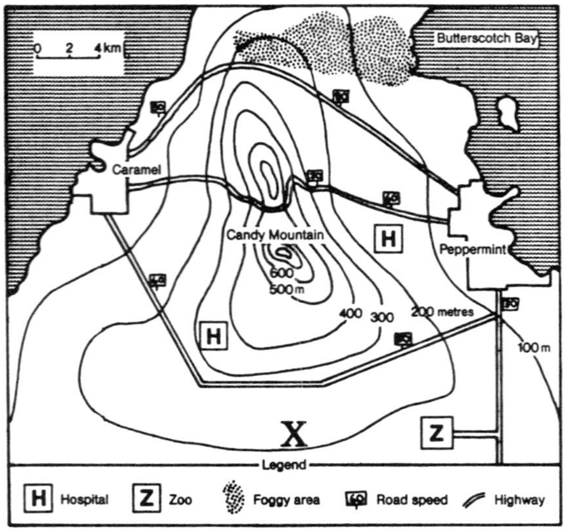

59. approx. 1400 km

60.

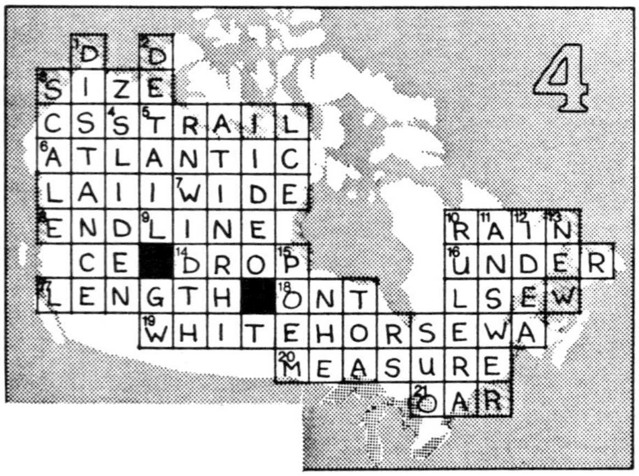

61. 1-river valley, 2-cliff, 3-mountain peak, 4-peninsula, 5-ridge, 6-delta, 7-river or stream

The remarkable progress in map-making techniques over the past 360 years is illustrated by the two maps on the cover of this book. The front cover shows a 1624 map of New France. The coastline of eastern Canada and New England is inaccurate, yet these land areas are still recognizable. Compare this map to the outline map of the same area on the back cover which was plotted and drawn by a Computer Aided Design and Drafting machine known as CADD.

CADD is capable of producing and manipulating sophisticated displays quickly at any scale or orientation with a high degree of precision. With CADD technology, engineers and planners no longer need to rely on less accurate, hand-drawn maps.

The CADD maps in this book were produced by Cole, Sherman & Associates Ltd., of Toronto; Consulting Engineers and Planners.

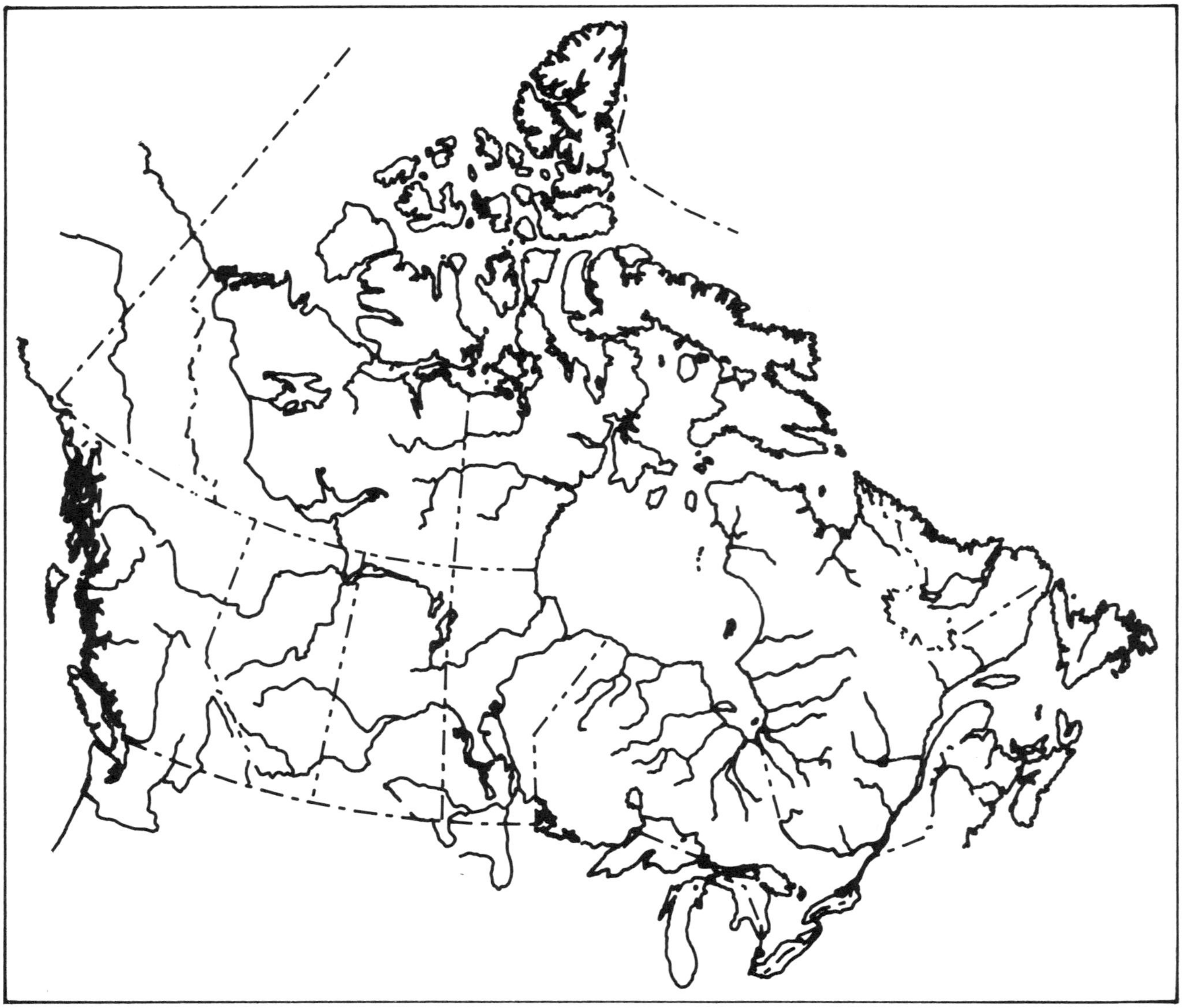